U0511897

《多彩中国节》丛书编委会
Editorial Committee of the Colorful Chinese Festivals Series

丛书主编 彭新良

The Water-Splashing Festival

汉英对照

泼水节

张跃 徐子珺 等 著

王艳芳 译

全国百佳图书出版单位

APTIME
时代出版

时代出版传媒股份有限公司
安徽人民出版社

图书在版编目（CIP）数据

泼水节：汉英对照 / 张跃，徐子珺等著；王艳芳译 . —— 合肥：安徽人民出版社，2018.8
（多彩中国节丛书 / 彭新良主编）

ISBN 978-7-212-10030-8

Ⅰ . ①泼… Ⅱ . ①张… ②徐… ③王… Ⅲ . ①傣族－民族节日－少数民族风俗习惯－中国－汉、英 Ⅳ . ① K892.1

中国版本图书馆 CIP 数据核字 (2018) 第 005262 号

《多彩中国节》丛书

泼水节：汉英对照
POSHUI JIE

彭新良　丛书主编
张跃　徐子珺 等　著　　　王艳芳　译

出版人：徐　敏　　　　　　　　选题策划：刘　哲　陈　娟
出版统筹：张　旻　袁小燕　　　责任编辑：郑世彦
责任印制：董　亮　　　　　　　装帧设计：陈　爽　宋文岚

出版发行：时代出版传媒股份有限公司 http://www.press-mart.com
　　　　　安徽人民出版社 http://www.ahpeople.com
地　　址：合肥市政务文化新区翡翠路 1118 号出版传媒广场八楼
邮　　编：230071
电　　话：0551-63533258　0551-63533259（传真）
印　　刷：安徽联众印刷有限公司

开本：880mm×1230mm　1/32　印张：7.875　字数：230 千
版次：2018 年 8 月第 1 版　　2018 年 9 月第 1 次印刷

ISBN　978-7-212-10030-8　　　　　　　定价：38.00 元

代 序

我们共同的日子

个人一年一度最重要的日子是生日,大家一年一度最重要的日子是节日。节日是大家共同的日子。

节日是一种纪念日,内涵多种多样。有民族的、国家的、宗教的,比如国庆节、圣诞节等。有某一类人的,如妇女、儿童、劳动者的,这便是妇女节、儿童节、劳动节等。也有与人们的生活生产密切相关的,这类节日历史悠久,很早就形成了一整套人们约定俗成、代代相传的节日习俗,这是一种传统的节日。传统节日也多种多样。中国是一个多民族国家,有 56 个民族,统称中华民族。传统节日有全民族共有的,也有某个民族特有的。比如春节、中秋节、元宵节、端午节、清明节、重阳节等,就为中华民族所共用和共享;世界文化遗产羌年就为羌族独有和独享。各民族这样的节日很多。

传统节日是在漫长的农耕时代形成的。农耕时代生产与生活、人与自然的关系十分密切。人们或为了感恩于大自然的恩赐,或为了庆祝辛勤劳作换来的收获,或为了激发生命的活力,或为了加强人际的亲情,经过长期相互认同,最终约定俗成,渐渐把一年中某一天确定为节日,并创造了十分完整又严格的节俗,如仪式、庆典、规制、禁忌,乃至特定的游艺、装饰与食品,来把节日这天演化成一个独具内涵、迷人的日子。更重要的是,人们在每一个传统的节日里,还把共同的生活理想、人间愿望与审

001

美追求融入节日的内涵与种种仪式中。因此,它是中华民族世间理想与生活愿望极致的表现。可以说,我们的传统——精神文化传统,往往就是依靠这代代相传的一年一度的节日继承下来的。

然而,自从 20 世纪整个人类进入由农耕文明向工业文明的过渡,农耕时代形成的文化传统开始瓦解。尤其是中国,在近百年由封闭走向开放的过程中,节日文化——特别是城市的节日文化受到现代文明与外来文化的冲击。当下人们已经鲜明地感受到传统节日渐行渐远,并为此产生忧虑。传统节日的淡化必然使其中蕴含的传统精神随之涣散。然而,人们并没有坐等传统的消失,主动和积极地与之应对。这充分显示了当代中国人在文化上的自觉。

近 10 年,随着中国民间文化遗产抢救工程的全面展开,国家非物质文化遗产名录申报工作的有力推动,传统节日受到关注,一些重要的传统节日被列入了国家文化遗产名录。继而,2006 年国家将每年 6 月的第二个周六确定为"文化遗产日",2007 年国务院决定将 3 个中华民族的重要节日——清明节、端午节和中秋节列为法定放假日。这一重大决定,表现了国家对公众的传统文化生活及其传承的重视与尊重,同时也是保护节日文化遗产十分必要的措施。

节日不放假必然直接消解了节日文化,放假则是恢复节日传统的首要条件。但放假不等于远去的节日立即就会回到身边。节日与假日的不同是因为节日有特定的文化内容与文化形式。那么,重温与恢复已经变得陌生的传统节日习俗则是必不可少的了。

千百年来,我们的祖先从生活的愿望出发,为每一个节日都创造出许许多多美丽又动人的习俗。这种愿望是理想主义的，所以节日习俗是理想的；愿望是情感化的，所以节日习俗也是情感化的；愿望是美好的，所以节日习俗是美的。人们用合家团聚的年夜饭迎接新年；把天上的明月化为手中甜甜的月饼，来象征人间的团圆；在严寒刚刚消退、万物复苏的早春，赶到野外去打扫墓地，告慰亡灵，表达心中的缅怀，同时戴花插柳，踏青春游，亲切地拥抱大地山川……这些诗意化的节日习俗，使我们一代代人的心灵获得了美好的安慰与宁静。

对于少数民族来说，他们特有的节日的意义则更加重要。节日还是他们民族集体记忆的载体、共同精神的依托、个性的表现、民族身份之所在。

谁说传统的习俗过时了？如果我们淡忘了这些习俗，就一定要去重温一下传统。重温不是表象地模仿古人的形式，而是用心去体验传统中的精神与情感。

在历史进程中，习俗是在不断变化的，但民族传统的精神实质不应变。这传统就是对美好生活的不懈追求，对大自然的感恩与敬畏，对家庭团圆与世间和谐永恒的企望。

这便是我们节日的主题，也是这套《多彩中国节》丛书编写的根由与目的。

中国56个民族是一个大家庭，各民族的节日文化异彩纷呈，既有春节、元宵节、中秋节这样多民族共庆的节日，也有泼水节、火把节、那达慕等少数民族特有的节日。这套丛书选取了中国最有代表性的10个传统节日，一节一册，图文并茂，汉英对照，旨在为海内外读者通俗、全面地呈现中国绚丽多彩的节庆文化和民俗文化；放在一起则是中华民族传统节日的一部全书，既有知识性、资料性、工具性，又有可读性和趣味性。10本精致的小册子,以翔实的文献和生动的传说,将每个节日的源起、流布与习俗,图文并茂、有滋有味地娓娓道来,从这些节日的传统中,可以看出中国人的精神追求和文化脉络。这样一套丛书不仅是对我国传统节日的一次总结,也是对传统节日文化富于创意的弘扬。

　　我读了书稿,心生欣喜,因序之。

冯骥才

（全国政协常委、中国文联原执行副主席）

Preface

Our Common Days

The most important day for a person is his or her birthday while the most important days for all are festivals, which are our common days.

Festivals are embedded with rich connotations for remembering. There're ethnic, national, and religious ones, such as National Day and Christmas Day; festivals for a certain group of people, such as Women's Day, Children's Day, and Laborers' Day; and those closely related to people's life and production, which enjoy a long history and feature a complete set of well-established festive traditions passed on from one generation to another. These are so-called traditional festivals, which vary greatly, too.

China, consisting of 56 nationalities, is a multi-ethnic country. People in China are collectively called the Chinese nation. So it's no wonder that some of the traditional festivals are celebrated by all nationalities while others only by certain nationalities, with the representatives of the former ones being the Spring Festival, the Lantern Festival, the Dragon Boat Festival, the Tomb-Sweeping Festival, and the Double Ninth Festival, etc. and that of the latter being the Qiang New Year, a unique festival for Qiang ethnic group. Each of ethnic groups in China has quite a number of their unique traditional festivals.

The traditional festivals have taken shape in the long agrarian times when people were greatly dependent on nature and when life was closely related to production. People gradually saw eye to eye with each other in the long-term practicing sets of rituals, celebrations, taboos as well as games, embellishments, and foods in a strict way and decided to select some days of one year as festivals with a view to expressing their gratitude to nature, celebrating harvesting, stimulating vitality of life, or strengthening bonds between family members and relatives. In this way, festivals have evolved into charming days with unique connotations. More importantly, people have instilled their common aspirations and aesthetic pursuits into festive connotations and rituals. To put it simply, festivals are consummate demonstrations of Chinese people's worldly aspirations and ideals, and Chinese people's spiritual cultures are inherited for generations by them.

Nevertheless, the cultural traditions formed in the agrarian times began to collapse with human beings being in transition from agrarian civilization to industrial one, esp., in China, whose festive cultures were severely hammered by modern civilization and foreign cultures in nearly one hundred years from being closed to opening up to the world. Nowadays, people strongly feel that traditional festivals are drifting away from their lives and are deeply concerned about it owing to the fact that dilution of traditional festivals means the fall of the traditional spirit of Chinese people. Of course, we don't wait and see; instead, we cope with it in a positive way. This fully displays the contemporary Chinese people's cultural consciousness.

In recent ten years, the traditional festivals have been earning more and more attention and some significant ones are included to the list of the National Heritages with the vigorous promotion of China's Folk Heritage Rescue Program and China's intangible cultural heritage application; for example, China set the second Saturday of June as "Cultural Heritage Day" in 2006; the State Council decided to list three significant traditional festivals as legal holidays—the Tomb-Sweeping Festival, the Dragon Boat Festival, and the Mid-Autumn Festival in 2007. These measures show the state gives priority to and pay tribute to the inheritance of public traditional cultures.

Holidays are necessary for spending festivals which will be diluted otherwise; however, holidays don't necessarily bring back traditional festivals. Since festivals, different from holidays, are equipped with special cultural forms and contents, it's essential to recover those traditional festive customs which have become stranger and stranger to contemporary Chinese people.

In the past thousands of years, our ancestors, starting from their aspirations, created many fine and engaging traditions. These aspirations are ideal, emotional, and beautiful, so are the festival traditions. People usher in the New Year by having the meal together on the New Year's Eve, make moon cakes by imitating the moon in the sky, standing for family reunion, or go to sweep the tombs of ancestors or family members for commemorating or comforting in the early spring when the winter just recedes and everything wakes up while taking spring hiking and enjoying spring scenes by the way. These poetic festive customs greatly comfort souls of people for generations.

As for ethnic minority people, their special festivals mean more to them. The festivals carry the collective memory, common spirit, character of their ethnic groups as well as mark their ethnic identities.

Are the traditional festive customs really out-dated? We're compelled to review them if we really forget them. What matters for review is not imitating the forms of the ancient Chinese people's celebrations but experiencing essence and emotions embedded in them with heart and soul.

Traditions have evolved with history's evolving, but the traditional national spirit has never changed. The spirit lies in people's never-ending pursuit for beautiful life, consistent gratitude and awe for nature, constant aspiration for family reunion and world harmony.

This is also the theme of our festivals and the root-cause of compiling the series.

The Chinese nation, featuring its colorful and varieties of festive cultures, boasts the common festivals celebrated by all nationalities, such as the Spring Festival, the Lantern Festival, the Mid-Autumn Festival, and the ethnic festivals, such as the Water Splashing Festival (Thai people), the Torch Festival (Yi people), Naadam (Mongolian nationality). This series, selecting the most typical ten festivals of China, with each festival being in one volume with figures and in both English and Chinese, unfolds the colorful festive and folk cultures in an engaging and all-round way for appealing to foreign readers. If put together, they constitute a complete set of books on Chinese traditional festivals, being instructive and intriguing. The ten brochures elaborate on the origins, distribution, and customs of each festival in an engaging way with figures, tales, and rich literature. Chinese people's spiritual pursuit and cultural veining can be tracked in this series, serving as a summary of Chinese traditional festivals and innovative promotion of them.

I went over the series with delight, and with delight, wrote the preface, too.

Feng Jicai

CPPCC National Committee member

Former Vice-president of the China Federation of Literary and Art Circles

目 录

多彩中国节

泼水节

Contents

引　言

　　从茫茫太空俯瞰,地球是一个闪耀着蓝色光芒的水球。水是这个星球分布最广泛的一种宝贵的自然资源,也是人类赖以生存的物质条件。水是生命之源,是孕育生命的母体和一切生命的依托,从一开始便与人类生活乃至文化历史形成了一种不解之缘。纵观世界文明源流,是水势滔滔的尼罗河孕育了灿烂的古埃及文明,是奔腾不息的幼发拉底河见证了巴比伦王国的盛衰兴亡,是蔚蓝美丽的地中海创造了绚烂多姿的古希腊文化,而流淌在东方的长江与黄河,则滋润了沿袭至今的中华文明。

　　水乃万物之源,论功勋当得起颂词千篇、丰碑万座。可它反而"和其光,同其尘",哪里低往哪里流,哪里洼在哪里聚,愈深邃愈安静。水一旦融为一体,肩并肩,手挽手,一个方向,一个步调,生死相依,没有什么力量能使它们分开。它们汇聚而成江海,浩浩淼淼,荡今涤古;它们乘风便起波涛,与土地结合,便是土地的一部分,与生命结合,便是生命的一部分;它们总是因时而变,夜结露珠,晨飘雾霭,晴蒸祥瑞,阴披霓裳;它们夏为雨,冬为雪,化而生气,凝而成冰。此等宁静达观,洋溢着谦谦君子之姿,和谐可爱,实在妙不可言。

　　老子有上善若水,水利万物而不争的豁达;孔子有仁智者乐水,仁者乐山,智者动,仁者静,智者乐,仁者寿的喟叹。水柔而能克刚,静而能印物,动而能变,与时俱进,此水之智也;牺牲自我,清洁万物,不争功、不诿过,滋养万物,孕育生命,此水之德也。在中国,水文化以各种各样的形式存在,泼水节便是其中最为典型也最被熟知的体现之一。"泼"在字典中的释意为"猛力倒水使散开:泼洒"。这个简单的动作在与"水"这一物质载体相结合,在被赋予了种种习俗礼节、文化信仰、经济活动之后,便自然而然地增加了多姿多彩的内涵与性质,成为了一个超越简单动作的文化符号,为不同民族民众所共享欢愉。

泼水节的英文名称为"*The Water-Splashing Festival*",源于印度,曾经是婆罗门教的一种宗教仪式。其后,为佛教所吸收,经缅甸传入中国。在中国,泼水节成为云南少数民族中影响面最大、参与人数最多的传统节日之一。除了最具代表性的傣族泼水节以外,这个节日对信仰南传佛教的阿昌族、德昂族、布朗族、佤族等也有着特殊的意义。不仅如此,泼水节也是泰语民族和东南亚地区的传统节日。泼水节当日,泰国、老挝、缅甸、柬埔寨等国,以及海外傣/泰人聚居地的人们清早起来便沐浴礼佛,之后开始连续几日的庆祝活动。期间,大家用纯净的清水相互泼洒,祈求洗去过去一年的不顺和灾祸。

由于泼水节的流布广泛,因此这个节日在不同国家和地区的不同民族中有不同称谓,例如,在中国云南省西双版纳和德宏地区的傣族分别称为"桑堪比迈"(意即新年)、"尚罕""尚键";德昂族称为"哄拍",意为"浴佛节";阿昌族则称"浇花水";泰国、老挝、柬埔寨等国叫"宋干";缅语则称为"摩诃丁键",意为"大过渡""大转移"。

各地区泼水节都有丰富多彩的活动内容,节日期间的主要活动有浴佛、诵经、赕佛、放生、泼水、跳孔雀舞、跳象脚鼓舞、放高升、放孔明灯、堆沙、丢包、赛龙舟、打陀螺、斗鸡等。泼水节还充分展示了各族人民丰富的服饰、饮食、宗教等文化与习俗,在中国节庆文化中展现了绚丽多彩的篇章。

○ 传统的傣族泼水（云南勐海）

Introduction

Viewed from the vast space, the earth is a bluish water ball. Water is the most widely distributed precious natural resource of the planet, and also a material condition for human survival. Water is the source of life, the matrix of life breeding and the support of all life; from the very beginning, it has formed a kind of indissoluble bound with human life and cultural history. Throughout the world cultural origins, it was the gushing waterflow of the Nile that gave birth to the brilliant ancient Egyptian civilization, the surging Euphrates that witnessed the rise and fall of the kingdom of Babylon, the beautiful blue Mediterranean that created the colorful ancient Greek culture, and the Yangtze River and Yellow River flowing in the east that have moistened the Chinese civilization up to now.

Water is the source of all things, and its feats are worthy of numerous eulogies and monuments. But it is "with its light, with its dust", flowing where it is low, gathering at the depressions, and the deeper it goes, the quieter it becomes. Once waters are integrated, they will work shoulder to shoulder, arm in arm, in one direction, in one step, sticking together in life and death with no power to separate them. They gather into rivers and sea, vast and misty, swinging the present and cleaning the past; embracing the wind, they can arouse waves; combining with the land, they become part of the land, and combining with life, they become part of the life; they always change with time, like the dew of the night and the mist in the morning; they become rain in summer and snow in winter, transforming into vapor or ice under different temperatures. These noble characters of tranquility, optimism and modesty are harmonious, lovely and fantastic.

Lao Zi praised the generosity of water with the saying that the top virtue is water, benefiting everything but striving for nothing. Confucius marveled that the wise love water, while the benevolent prefer mountains; the wise enjoy activities, while the benevolent remain quiet; the wise are happy, while the benevolent live long. Water is soft but can overcome firmness; it is quiet but can affect other things; it can move and change, and keep pace with the time; this is the wisdom of water. Water can sacrifice itself to clean all things; it is uncompetitive, does not shift the blame, nourishes all things, and breeds life; this is the virtue of water. In China, water culture also exists in a variety of forms, and the Water-Splashing Festival is one of the most typical and well-known representations. "Splash" in the dictionary means "to pour the water to disperse". This simple action, after combining with the material carrier of "water" and being endowed with a variety of custom etiquette, cultural belief and economic activities, has been naturally added colorful connotations and character, and become a cultural symbol beyond simple action shared by different peoples.

The English name "the Water-Splashing Festival" originated from India, which was once a religious ritual of Brahmanism. Later it was absorbed by Buddhism and introduced into China via Burma. In China, it has become one of the most influencial and most participated traditional festivals in minorities of

Yunnan Province. In addition to the most representative Dai Water-Splashing Festival, this festival also has a special meaning to Achang, De'ang, Bulang and Vanationality that believe in Southern Sect of Buddhism. Besides, Water-Splashing Festival is also a traditional festival of Thai ethnic groups and Southeast Asia. On the day of the festival, people in Thailand, Laos, Burma, Cambodia, and overseas Dai/Thai groups rise early in the morning, bathe themselves and pay respect to the Buddha, and then start the celebrations lasting for several days. During the period, people splash clean water on each other, praying to wash away the misfortunes of the past year.

As a result of the wide spread of the Water-Splashing Festival, it has different names in different ethnic groups of different countries and regions. For example, the Dai nationality of Xishuangbanna and Dehong region in Yunnan Province of China respectively call it "Sangkan Bimai" (ie, New Year), "Shanghan" or "Shangjian"; De'ang nationality calls it "Hongpai", meaning "Festival of Bathing the Buddha"; Achang nationality calls it "Flower-watering Festival"; Thailand, Laos and Cambodia call it "Songkran"; it is called "Mohedingjian" in the Burmese language, meaning "great transition" or "great shift".

There are rich and colorful activities to celebrate the Water-Splashing Festival in different regions, mainly including bathing the Buddha, chanting sutras, Danfo (offering sacrifice to the Buddha), freeing captive animals, splashing water, dancing Peacock Dance, dancing Elephant-foot Drum Dance, letting off Gaosheng, flying Kongming lanterns, piling up sand, tossing embroidered parcels, dragon boat racing, whipping tops, cockfighting and so on. The Water-Splashing Festival also fully presents different ethnic groups' rich culture and customs of costume, dietand religion, unfolding a colorful picture of Chinese festival culture.

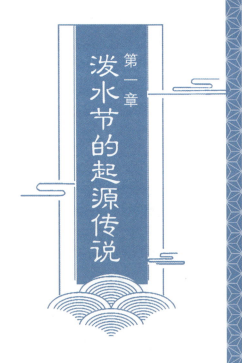

泼水节，这个富有悠久历史内涵和浪漫色彩的节日，就像有关它的故事和传说一样神秘、动人，令人陶醉，令人向往。泼水节源于印度，约在公元 12 世纪末至 13 世纪初经缅甸传入中国云南傣族地区，距今已有 800 多年历史。而随着南传佛教影响的增大，泼水节的习俗也日益丰富。在中国，除了傣族人民在每年的傣历新年期间庆祝之外，其他有些民族也有着过泼水节的传统。

不同的地区有着不同的物候变迁，从而造就了各地民众对事物的不同理解，节日也是这样。由于泼水节在不同国家和地区发展，并与当地文化相结合而出现了差异。在有关泼水节的起源和传说方面，不同国家和不同民族既有着不同的传统和解释，也有着相应的继承和发展。现在，不妨让我们一起回望泼水节那遥远的传说源头，一睹它浪漫而神秘的动人风采。

一、
"七女捧头"的传说

据说远古时候，没有天地，没有万物，茫茫的太空中滚动着气体、烟雾，呼呼地刮着狂风。不知过了多少年，气体夹着烟雾，狂风吹拂着气体，夹着吹着、吹着夹着，这三样东西终于凝结成一个巨大的人形，这个人形后来便成为创造天地和万物的英叭神。英叭神的智慧和神力无比，可以创造万物。有了万物之后，英叭神便派天神叭奔去安排季节和节令，掌管天地气象，按照天规行云播雨，调控阴晴。谁料他自恃神通广大，无视天规，不分季节，不推日子，一切都率性而为。春耕时，他来个骄阳似火，不刮风不降雨，弄得土地龟裂，禾苗枯竭；秋收时节，他又大雨滂沱，洪水泛滥，搞得人间颗粒无收，灾难重重。英叭神闻讯悔恨不已，决定亲自出马收拾这个无法无天的恶神。

英叭神变成一个英俊的小伙子，潜入叭奔家里，动员他的七个女儿："你们的父亲是个恶神，他违犯天规乱兴风雨，给人间造成了大灾大难。你们谁能为民除害，我就娶她为妻。"七个女儿本来就对父亲早怀不满，如今更想除掉他为黎民百姓消灾。她们千方百计亲近父亲，打探他的生死秘诀。而叭奔终于在一次酒后吐露了他害怕自己头发的秘密。七个女儿乘父亲酣睡时剪下他的一络头发，做成置他于死地的"弓箭栽"。最小的七姑娘把"弓箭栽"对准父亲的脖颈祈祷："如果父亲违犯天规，残害黎民百姓，那就让他死在今天。"话音刚落，叭奔的脖颈就被头发割断。当他的头颅滚落地上时，便四处燃烧，冒出熊熊烈火；抛向天空，则天旱不雨；丢入海里，则海水干涸。七姑娘只得急忙把那头颅抱在怀里，说来也怪，冒着烈火的头颅一到她的怀里就烟灭火熄。于是，为避免父亲的头颅起火生灾，七个女儿便轮流把它抱在怀里，一年一换，每365天为一周年，七女按次序轮换，直到它腐烂为止，并在每次轮换时用清水泼洒冲洗身上的污渍。

恶神清除后，英叭神重修天历，推算日子降雨刮风，按照季节播热放冷。从此，人间风调雨顺，五谷丰登。新的历法于傣历六月传到人间，由此，傣家人就把六月以前称为旧岁，六月以后称作新年，在每年六月份欢度新年佳节。人们为纪念大义灭亲、为人间消灾的七位仙女，也学着她们那样每年进行泼水祝福。从此，便传下了过年泼水的习俗。

这个传说在不同地区出现了多种类似"变体"，消除恶魔的主体有的也被表述为"妻子"。总之，后来为了纪念也为了怀念，每到新年这一天，人们便会相互泼水，以此来浇灭心中的"火"，洗去身体与心灵的污垢，祝福在新的一年里消灾弭祸、身体健康。今天的泼水习俗，已由原先的轻扬树枝蘸水相洒以示祝福，演变成全民端盆提桶的泼水狂欢。城镇的大街小巷，乡间的村村寨寨，到处鼓乐喧天，银花飞溅，欢声笑语四处荡漾。

从传说可以看出，泼水的目的，主要是洗去捧着"天神"或者"魔王"的头颅染在姑娘身上的污血，具有洗掉一切污秽、疾病和灾难的意义，使得人们身心洁净。水是吉祥之物，能洗去烦恼，带走疾病灾祸，为人们带来吉祥幸福。泼水节期间的相互泼水，也隐含了吉祥的蕴意，那就是：水是吉祥之物，水能冲走疾病灾难，带来健康幸福。

○泼出幸福之水（云南景洪）

二、
"李良救火"的传说

关于泼水节的来历，在金沙江河谷的傣族村落中则有这样一个传说。

很早以前，傣家人为躲避战乱，从景东、景谷迁到金沙江畔一带。那时，东山盘踞着神龙之子仁凉（即干龙），江河里居住着仁南（即水龙）。傣族人逃到这里后，仁凉想方设法加以伤害。有一年正值春耕大忙之时，仁凉从天上投下神火，傣家村寨顿时卷入火海之中。这时，一个英俊的"卜冒"（意为小伙子）李良，光着脚板，赤着胳臂，提起水桶飞快地跑向江边提水灭火。在他的带动下，男女老幼都提起竹桶到金沙江打水灭火。李良虽然已劳累过度，但他仍将竹桶捆在背上，不停地向前爬去，鲜血染红了沿路的石头。正当他解下水桶向大火泼去时，却被大火吞没了。瞬间，电闪雷鸣，下了一场大雨，把大火泼熄了，山寨也变成了一个小湖泊。水干后，寨子中间出现一棵大树，树梢上挂着李良的遗体。傣家男女老少都在悲哭，大树说："我是仁南，是李良的行为感动了我。今后傣家人不会再受苦了。"说完抱着李良的遗体腾身飞进了金沙江。

从此，傣族人民为了纪念李良，也为了纪念他为民除害的勇敢精神，每年清明前，每家房屋都要清扫一新，用绿树搭起长 500 米的青棚，两旁放上盛满水的水槽。午间太阳当顶的时候，众人穿行于青棚下相互用松枝蘸水洒身，表示对李良的怀念和对新年的祝福。这项活动延续至今，成为了金沙江沿岸傣族人民辞旧迎新、祝福吉祥的泼水节。

那些威力无穷的"天神"和"恶魔"是强有力的大自然的代表，而与之斗争的人类正是同自然危害做斗争的英雄。这个传说显示了远古人类征服自然的勇气和精神，反映了各民族先民早期的朴素意识。

三
傣历历法说

另一个传说与傣历的创立和形成有关。

在佛祖未成佛之前，人类共居，无人领导。于是人们共同商议，推选"佛祖"为长者，管理人类。佛祖看到当时的人类没有历法，便根据气候变化，制订历法。一年 12 个月，有大小月之分，大月 30 天，小月 29 天。但太上老君认为此法不当，应该订为每年 13 个月，每月 30 天。两人争论，相持不下，遂以砍头为赌注。结果，太上老君所订的历法施行数年，不合季节，于是便砍头以实践诺言。但是，头落地后，便会发生火灾。佛祖便命令自己的七个女儿，每人轮流抱头一天。天上一天，地上一年。每年移交人头时，必须用水洗去血迹，以免污血滴到人间，发生灾害。故每年都要泼水一次。

除了傣族，在布朗族民间，也世世代代传唱着一个古老的故事。

巨神及其十二个孩子创造了天地和万物。太阳九姊妹和月亮十弟兄齐出，巨神造弓箭射落八个太阳和九个月亮，避免了万物被曝晒而死。但是，剩下的一个太阳姐姐和一个月亮哥哥却吓得躲藏了起来，人世间一片黑暗，寒冷不堪。巨神召集百鸟百兽去请他们，让荧火虫照亮，燕子带路。巨神自己不出面，怕吓着了日、月二位。

百鸟百兽找到了日、月藏身的山洞，让公鸡与他们订了协议：白天太阳出来，晚上月亮出来。

所以，在泼水节时，布朗人要在太阳出山前于村寨东边搭建一个彩棚。人们穿戴整齐，在供案上摆放糯米、酒、肉、芭蕉等，由寨老主持迎接日出。人们迎着东方喷薄而出的旭日，载歌载舞，感谢太阳给人间以温暖，给万物以生机，当然也忘不了巨神的功劳。早饭之后，人们还要结队到佛寺去堆沙塔、插花、浴佛，并泼水祝福。

从神话传说可以看出，按照正确的历法行事就可以驱除干旱、助天降雨，以便为即将来临的农业生产提供充沛的雨水。为了获得更好的收成，人们求助于神灵，因此就出现了祭祀各种神灵的仪式。可以说，这些神话传说正是远古人类崇拜大自然的古朴思想的体现和原始宗教思想的遗风。

○飞扬的激情（云南勐腊）

虽然关于泼水节起源的各种版本故事情节略有差距，但是它们都有比较明显的共同点，即都提到了"干旱"和"雨水"。说到泼洒清水的原因，几乎都提及了砍头、七女捧头。由此可见，关于泼水节起源的不同传说，一方面是通过文学形式歌颂和赞扬远古人类征服大自然的伟大精神和成果；另一方面则反映了不同民族的历史传统、地理环境、生计方式、生活条件及其民族心理。东南亚中南半岛的泰国、缅甸、老挝、柬埔寨等国家以及中国傣族地区都处在亚热带区域，虽然雨量充沛，但是常年气候炎热，尤其是到了傣历的4～5月份，是一年中最为炎热的季节。相同的地域环境产生了相似的习俗和文化类型，人们以泼水的形式庆祝新年，不仅能够消除炎热、获得清凉，同时也祈求降雨，以便于即将来临的农忙耕种。于是以此为背景，便衍生出了独特的节日习俗，也就此产生了相应的神话传说。

Chapter One
The Legends of the Water-Splashing Festival

The Water—Splashing Festival, which is rich in historical connotation and romantic glamour, just like the stories and legends around it, is mysterious, appealing, intoxicating and desirable.It originated from India and was introduced to the regions of Dai nationality in Yunnan Province of China from the end of the 12th century to the early 13th century. Till now it has had a history of more than 800 years. And with the increasing influence of the Southern Sect of Buddhism, the customs of this festival are increasingly abundant. In China, in addition to Dai people's celebrating it during Dai New Year, some other ethnic groups also have a tradition of celebrating this festival.

Different regions have different phenological changes, which lead to people's different understanding of things in different regions. The same is true of festivals. Because the Water—Splashing Festival has developed in different countries and regions, its customers differ when it combines with the local culture. On the origins and legends of this festival, different countries and different nationalities have not only different traditions and interpretations, but also

corresponding inheritance and development. Now, let's look back at the distant sources of the Water-Splashing Festival and see its romantic and mysterious demeanour.

1. The Legend of "Seven Daughters Holding the Head"

It is said that in ancient times, there was no heaven, no earth, and nothing existed. In the vast space gas and smoke were rolling, and the wind was blowing hard. Numerous years passed, gas mixed up with smog, and the wild wind blew gas. Mixing and blowing, blowing and mixing, these three things finally condensed into a huge human form, which later became God Ying Ba who created the heaven, the earth and all things. God Ying Ba had unusual wisdom and divine power, and could create all things. After creating everything, God Ying Ba sent for God Ba Ben to arrange for seasons and festivals, control the weather and regulate rain or shine according to heavenly rules. Unexpectedly, counting on his great power, Ba Ben defied the rules of the heaven, confusing the seasons, calculating no days and doing everything casually and carelessly. During spring ploughing, he produced a scorching heat, with no wind and no rain, and the soil cracked and the seedlings dried up. During the autumn harvest, however, he produced a heavy downpour; the flood destroyed the harvest, and disasters predominated. God Ying Ba regretted so much that he decided to take up the matter himself and punish this lawless evil god.

God Ying Ba turned into a handsome young man, slipped into Ba Ben's home, and mobilized his seven daughters, "Your father is an evil god. He violated heavenly rules to mess with wind and rain, which caused catastrophic damage to the human world. Whoever of you can kill him, I will marry her." The seven daughters, who were already dissatisfied with their father, now even more wanted to kill him for the sake of people. They tried to approach their father and explore his secret of life and death. And at last, he confided after drinking that he was afraid of his hair. The seven daughters, in their father's deep sleep, cut off a lock of his hair and made a "bow sieve fall" that could kill him. The youngest daughter prayed with the "bow sieve fall" pointing at their father's neck, "If our father broke the heavenly rules and did harm to the people, let him die today." As soon as she finished this sentence, Ba Ben's neck was cut off by his hair. When his head fell onto the ground, it burnt with raging flames; when it was cast into the sky, it would not rain; and when it was thrown into the sea, the water would dry up. In haste, the youngest daughter had to hold the head in her arms. Strangely, the smoke and fire extinguished as soon as the burning head reached into her arms. So, to avoid their father's head inducing a fire disaster, the seven daughters took turns to hold it in their arms. They changed shifts once a day, an anniversary for every 365 days. The seven daughters held the head in turn until it decayed, and they splashed and flushed the stain on them with clean water in each shift.

After the evil god was killed, God Ying Ba reset the heavenly calendar, calculated the days for rain and wind, and let out heat and cold according to the season. From then on, wind and rain came on time, and good harvests were produced. New calendar was introduced to the human world in June of Dai calendar. Thus, Dai people call the days before June the Old Year, the days after June the New Year, and celebrate the New Year festival in every June. In order to memorize the seven fairies who had placed righteousness above family loyalty and eliminated the evil in the world, people learnt from them to splash water for blessings every year. Since then, the custom of splashing water when celebrating the New Year has been handed down.

This legend has experienced a variety of similar variations in different regions, with the one killing the monster also being described as "wives". Anyhow, later to commemorate and also to remember, on every New Year's day, people will splash water on each other in order to extinguish the "fire" in heart, wash away the dirt from the body and soul, wish to eliminate the evil and keep healthy in the New Year. Today's splashing custom has evolved from the former splashing water for blessing by lightly raising branches dipped in water into a public carnival with people's pouring water by carrying basins and buckets. The big streets and small alleys of towns, villages and stockades of the countryside, all ring with cheers and laughter, with loud music filling the air.

As can be seen from the legend, the purpose of splashing water is mainly to wash away the grimy blood that the head of "God" or "Devil" dyed on the girls, which has the meaning of washing away all the filth, diseases and disasters, and making people clean in body and soul. Water is an auspicious thing, which can wash away worries, take away diseases and disasters, and bring auspicious happiness to people. Splashing water on each other during the Water-Splashing Festival also implies the auspicious meaning, namely, water is an auspicious thing, which can wash away diseases and disasters, and bring health and happiness.

2. The Legend of "Li Liang Putting out the Fire"

About the origin of the Water-Splashing Festival, there is such a legend in Dai villages around the Jinsha River Valley.

Legend has it that Dai people moved from Jingdong and

Jinggu to the border of Jinsha River to escape warfare long ago. At that time, the Dongshan Mountain was occupied by the Great Dragon's son, Ren Liang (ie. Dry Dragon), and the rivers were inhabited by Ren Nan (ie. Water Dragon). When Dai people fled here, Ren Liang tried to hurt them. One year during the busy spring ploughing, Ren Liang droped Great Fire from the sky, and immediately the Dai village was caught in fire. At this time, a handsome "Pu Mao" (meaning a young man), Li Liang, with bare feet and bare arms, lifted the bucket, and ran quickly to the river to fetch water to put out the fire. In his lead, all the people, without reference to age and sex, seized the bamboo buckets to fetch water in the Jinsha River. Although Li Liang was exhausted, he still bundled the bamboo bucket on his back and kept crawling forward, and the stones along the road were dyed red by his blood. Just as he was undoing the bucket to splash towards the fire, he was engulfed in it. In a flash, lightning flashed and thunder rumbled, and a heavy rain poured down. The fire was extinguished, and the village became a small sea. When the water became dry, a big tree appeared in the middle of the stockade, with the remains of Li Liang hanging from the treetops. All the Dai people were crying sadly when the tree said, "I am Ren Nan. It is Li Liang's action that has touched me. Dai people will not suffer any more in the future." With that, he flew into the Jinsha River holding Li Liang's body.

Since then, in order to commemorate Li Liang and his brave spirit to get rid of the evil for the people, Dai people have cleaned their houses before Tomb-sweeping Day, and have set up a cyan shed of 500 meters long with green trees, with tanks filled with water on both sides. At the peak of the noon sun, people walk through the shed while dipping pine branches in the water to splash each other, which is a way to express their yearning for Li Liang and blessings for the New Year. This activity continues till today, and has become the Water-Splashing Festival when Dai people along the Jinsha River ring out the Old Year and ring in the New Year and express auspicious blessings.

This legend represents the courage and spirit of the ancient humans to conquer nature. Those "God" and "Devil" with boundless power are representatives of powerful nature, while the humans fighting against them are heroes against natural hazards, which reflects the early sense of simplicity of the ethnic ancestors.

3. The Legend According to Dai Calendar

Another legend relates to the creation and formation of the Dai calendar.

Before the Lord Buddha's enlightenment, human beings lived together without any leaders. So people consulted together and elected the Lord Buddha to be the elder to manage the people. Seeing that there was no calendar for humans, the Lord Buddha formulated a calendar based on climate changes. There were twelve months in one year, with the big month of 30 days and the small month of 29 days.But Senior Moral thought that this method was improper, and every year should include 13 months and 30 days for each month. The two men argued and could not persuade each other, so they made a bet with the stake of beheading. As a result, the calendar by Senior Moral was proved not to be in season after implement for many years, so his head was cut to keep his promise. However, when the head hit the ground, there would be a fire. So the Lord Buddha ordered his seven daughters to hold the head in turn, each for one day. And one day in heaven corresponded to one year on the earth. Every year when the head was turned over, the blood must be washed with water to prevent the blood that would cause disasters from dripping into the human world. Therefore people would splash water every year.

In addition to Dai nationality, there is also an ancient story passed from generation to generation in Bulang nationality.

The Great God and his twelve children created the heaven, the earth and all things. The nine sisters of sun family and the ten brothers of moon family came out together. And the Great God made the bow and arrows to shoot down eight suns and nine moons, preventing things from being exposed to death. But the remaining sun sister and moon brother were frightened and went into hiding, which made the world dark and cold. The Great God then summoned hundreds of birds and beasts to invite them, with let glowworms illuminating and swallows leading the way. The Great God himself did not turn up in order not to scare the sun and the moon. The birds and beasts found the cave where the sun and moon were hiding, and let the rooster have a deal with them: the sun came out during the day while the moon came out at night.

Therefore, during the Water-Splashing Festival, Bulang people would set up a decorated tent in the east of the village before the sun rises. People dress neatly and put glutinous rice, wine, meat and banana on the altar table, and then under the host of the headman, people greet the rising sun. Against the sun bursting out from the east, people, singing and dancing, thank the sun for bringing warmth to the human world and life to all things. Of course, the contribution of the Great God cannot be forgotten. After breakfast, people would go to the Buddhist temple in line to pile up the sand tower, insert flowers, bathe the Buddha, and splash water for blessings.

As can be seen from the myths and legends, acting according to the correct calendar can remove drought and help with the rain to provide abundant rainwater for the forthcoming agricultural production. In order to get a better harvest, people turned to the gods. So there was a ritual of making offerings to the gods. So to speak, these mythological legends are the embodiment of ancient humans' simple thought on worshipping nature and the legacy of primitive religious ideas.

Although the plots of various versions about the origin of the Water-Splashing Festival have slight differences, they have obviously something in common, namely, they all mention "drought" and "rain". Speaking of the reason of splashing water, almost all of them mention the beheading and the seven daughters' holding the head. Thus, different legends about the origin of the Water-Splashing Festival, on the one hand, eulogize and praise the great spirit and achievement of ancient humans' conquering the nature through the form of literature; on the other hand, they reflect the historical traditions, geographical conditions, means of livelihood, living conditions and national psychology of different minorities. Countries like Thailand, Burma, Laos, and Cambodia in Indo-China Peninsula of Southeast Asia and Dai nationality areas in China are in the subtropical zone. Although the rainfall in these areas is abundant, the climate is very hot all the year round, especially in April and May of the Dai calendar, which is the hottest season of the year. The same geographical environment has produced similar customs and cultures. People celebrate the New Year in the form of splashing water, which can not only eliminate the scorching heat and bring refreshing cool, but also pray for rain for ease of the upcoming busy farming cultivation. In this context, the unique festival custom has been developed, and thus the corresponding myths and legends are generated.

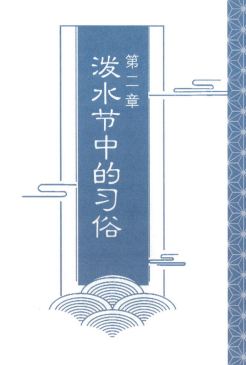

第二章

泼水节中的习俗

　　民族传统节日是各民族在其历史长河中为适应生产实践和社会生活而逐渐形成的，是集民俗事项、经贸活动、文娱竞技等于一体的文化事项，在不同程度上反映了该民族的社会历史、宗教信仰、生活方式和心理素质等。

　　"泼水节"是傣族等民族传统文化的"活化石"，神话传说、民族信仰、传统服饰、优美舞蹈和乡村集市在节日活动中被保留下来。"泼水节"不但反映着这些民族的宗教信仰和美好祝福，同时还是宗教文化、服饰文化、饮食文化、婚俗文化、歌舞文化、娱乐文化的大展演。

　　泼水节期间水雾弥漫，少数民族男女老少穿上节日盛装，沉浸在祝福的氛围里，互相泼洒，尽情尽兴，欢声笑语，锣鼓喧天，彩旗招展，人山人海，每一朵激溅的水花像幸福的笑脸盛开其间，热情四溅，祝福溢满。水泼得越多，祝福的呼声越高，爱情在望，力量蓄满，舞蹈鲜活，花火闪烁，一年更比一年好。

每一滴水注入无限的诚意，把象征平安健康、吉祥如意的祝福挥洒人间，传递着最原始纯粹美好的情谊祝愿。

○大家一起泼（云南景洪）

说起泼水节，首先就会联想到傣族。泼水节不仅是傣族最隆重的节日，也是云南少数民族节日中影响面最大、参加人数最多的节日之一。时至今日，泼水节的仪式和内容已发生了很大变化，但祈福和娱乐的核心功能被保留了下来。

一
神圣的宗教信仰

　　傣族是一个具有悠久历史和灿烂文化的民族，不仅有本民族的语言，还有自己的文字。傣族信奉的巴利语系佛教带有全民性，因此佛教建筑遍及傣家村寨。佛寺、佛塔建筑典雅精致，充分体现出傣族的宗教信仰。再加之灿烂的文学艺术，为佛寺壁画提供了优秀的创作题材，景洪就享有"线条造型美的世界"之盛名。傣族人民在佛寺壁画创作中，既见长于独创，又善于吸收和借鉴其他民族的优秀艺术，以情造线，以线传情，吸收别人的长处以充实自己，从而使佛寺壁画艺术更加绚丽多姿，成为傣族艺术宝库中的奇葩。在泼水节中，人们通过浴佛、诵经和堆沙等方式表达着他们对佛教的虔诚和坚定。

　　浴佛是最能体现信仰南传上座部佛教民众仪式尊崇的行为之一。

　　"浴佛"就是给佛像沐浴，包含洗礼的意思。傣族向佛、敬佛、礼佛，以善心慈行立身处世。佛在傣族人的心中，永远是那么庄严，那么圣洁，那么慈悲。为什么要给佛像沐浴呢？原来，在一心向佛的傣家人看来，即使是至高无上、佛法无边的佛，在一年中也难免有脱不了尘俗的时候，所以必须由凡人帮助佛像洗去一年中在人间沾染上的凡尘俗垢。因而在每年的傣历新年，傣家人都要举行隆重的"浴佛"仪式。

傣历新年一般有三天。第一天叫"宛麦"。这一天，各家各户都要认真打扫卫生，拆洗被褥，干干净净地迎接新年。第二天叫"宛恼"，是空日，意思是既不计算在旧年之内，也不计算在新年之内。第三天，傣语为"麦帕雅宛玛"，即"日子王"来到人间的那一天。这一天是傣家人举行"浴佛"仪式及盛大节日"泼水节"的开始。当天凌晨，所有傣族妇女都要起个大早，把清洁的井水或泉水挑到佛寺里，在太阳出来的时候，给佛像清洗尘埃。

傣族"浴佛"仪式非常肃穆和庄重。他们要在清洁的井水或泉水中，掺上各种美丽馨香的鲜花，采下青碧似玉的芭蕉叶，舀起圣洁的净水，小心翼翼地清洗擦拭，直至整座佛像金光灿烂，纤尘不染。说是"洗佛"，其实每一个傣家人都在"洗心"，在专心致志地除去自己心灵中的各种尘埃与污垢，把自己的心扉清洗得纯洁透亮，用虔诚重现佛像金碧辉煌的本色，以此祈求神灵保佑，祈祷来年吉祥平安。

诵经是最重要的仪式活动之一，不可缺少。

泼水节期间，年轻人可以参加跳舞、泼水、丢包、赛龙舟等活动，但是傣族老人的活动主要就是聚集在寺庙里面念经诵佛，或者是听寺庙里的佛爷念经。一般早晨 7:00 在家里洗漱，更换好新衣服之后，便会拿着前一天晚上采回来的鲜花到寺庙里面拜佛。也有老人说唱表演（说唱是最受傣族老人欢迎的一种表演，表演者需要根据自己在生活中所观察到的事情即兴说唱，一般是讲故事）。

堆沙活动也是傣族节日期间的一种风俗。

人们在佛寺的院子里用沙子堆成三座或五座金塔，塔高有一米多，上面插上几根缠着红绿布条的竹枝。然后，人们围坐在沙塔的四周，听和尚或佛爷诵经，祈求佛祖保佑在新的一年里风调雨顺、五谷丰收。现在"堆沙"变成了一种增进人们相互了解、和睦相处、团结友爱的民间娱乐或体育活动。堆沙通常在河边举行，是为了祈祷获得幸福与欢乐，避免灾难和痛苦。

○泼水节中的颂佛仪式（云南耿马）

佛教文化在傣族中影响深远。西双版纳的傣族是一个全民信教的民族，而且信的都是佛教中的南传上座部佛教，亦称小乘佛教。据传西双版纳地区的南传上座部佛教是由一位叫阿朱打拉西的人传进来的，至今已有1000多年的历史。傣族称宗教为"沙煞纳"，把他们信仰的佛教叫做"沙煞纳帕召戈达麻"。帕召戈达麻指的就是佛教教主乔达摩·悉达多——

○节日中的傣族小僧侣（云南耿马）

023

释迦牟尼。佛教文化随着历史的发展已经慢慢渗透进傣族人民的生活各方面，在泼水节这样隆重的节庆中人们更是无不表达自己的虔诚。

二
欢快的泼水仪式

水对于傣族民众有重要意义。水是吉祥之物，它能洗去烦恼，带走疾病灾祸，为人们带来吉祥幸福，为自己在新的一年里带来吉祥如意，泼水节期间泼水活动是最热闹和最传统的方式了。它不仅隐含了互相祝福的吉祥意义，而且随着时间的发展变得更热闹更多样了。每到泼水节，鼓锣之声响彻云霄，祝福的水花到处飞溅，人们一边翩翩起舞，一边呼喊"水！水！水！"，互相泼洒，互祝吉祥、幸福、健康，场面真是十分壮观！

每民族都有自己的习俗，每一个习俗都蕴含此民族的特殊寓意，表达了独特的智慧结晶和精神力量。泼水节作为傣族的神圣节日，其中水被看作一种具有生命力、生殖力的物质，直接表现了傣族人对它的崇拜，成为傣族社会生活中的神圣之物。男女老少，不分贵贱，都尽情享受着节日的欢乐。泼水是泼水节最主要的传统活动，泼水活动在泼水节的第二天达到最高潮。泼水的方式有多种，主要分为传统的泼水方式和现代的泼水方式。傣族传统的泼水方式又分为文泼和武泼。现代的泼水方式主要集中在一些城市或者各民族混杂共同欢度泼水节的地区，主要表现为多元文化互动下的活动方式。

○快乐的傣族少女（云南景洪）

（一）传统泼水方式

傣族传统的泼水方式分为"文泼"和"武泼"。

文泼就是傣家人到井里取来干净的水，要在水中泡上花瓣和贝叶。花瓣主要用的是茉莉花、月季花、玫瑰花的花瓣，这些花瓣浸泡在清水里会让水有香味。贝叶是佛教徒用来抄写佛经的树叶，可以驱鬼辟邪。节日泼上这样圣洁的水，象征着吉祥和幸福。人们提着盛有花香味的清水到寺庙里，用这些带有芳香的水给佛像清洗身上的灰尘，之后大家互相用嫩绿的小树枝蘸取小盆里或小水桶里的香花水，首先向德高或年长者身上轻轻洒去，再向年轻的人或者自己想要祝福的人身上洒去。洒水的量很少，就像春天的蒙蒙细雨，一般不会清透人们身上的衣衫。如此温柔地泼洒着带有淡淡花香味的清泉水，傣家人表达的是对他人和自己在新年里最真诚和美好的祝愿。

025

武泼是青年们喜欢的形式，通常只泼同辈的年轻人。武泼的形式没有一定的讲究，可以用大盆、大桶盛上水向对方头脸或身上泼洒，对方也可以用同样的方式互相追逐还击。按照傣族的传统文化，新年互相泼水象征着祝福和友谊，凡是参加泼水活动的人，都是乐意接受别人泼水的，被泼得越多越高兴。傣家人常说："一年一度泼水节，看得起谁就泼谁。"在傣族新年的泼水活动中，不管生人、熟人、傣族人或外地人，凡是来参加活动的人都会受到热烈的欢迎与祝福。

○ 乐在其中（云南芒市）

（二）现代泼水方式

随着泼水节的影响力越来越大，它覆盖了云南的许多城市与乡村。现在，城市里的汉族民众和其他民族的人也会参与到泼水的大军当中。例如，在昆明市的云南民族村里，每年的傣历新年（公历4月13日到15日），都会有很多来自全国各地的游客参与泼水节活动。他们提着大桶的水、抬着大盆的水或者拿着各式各样的盛水器具，见人就泼。泼水节拉近了陌生人之间的距离。

泼水节在城市里面展现的是一种狂欢，可能有人觉得野蛮而无法接受，有人则觉得痛快而比较崇尚，但在不同泼水方式中能感受的是人们的热情和相互浓烈的祝福。你泼我，我泼你，一朵朵水花在空中盛开，它象征着吉祥、幸福、健康，青年泼出的明亮晶莹的水珠，还象征着甜蜜的爱情。大家互相泼啊泼，到处是水的洗礼、水的祝福、水的欢歌。

○欢乐的人群（云南瑞丽）

旅游小贴士

西双版纳泼水广场

泼水节是西双版纳傣族的新年，是傣家最隆重的节日，会有赛龙舟、放高升和孔明灯、泼水狂欢和赶摆等活动，其中丢包、民族歌舞和斗鸡是民族风情中比较重要的内容。泼水节期间，身着民族服饰的当地民众和外地游客集聚在西双版纳州景洪市泼水广场互相泼水。泼水广场是景洪的中心地标建筑，也是每年泼水节期间的主会场；位于景洪市南过境路边上，靠近澜沧江及傣江南夜市。广场中间的喷水池和前面的塑像体现了泼水节的元素。每年四五月间如果亲临现场，就能感受那种热火朝天的泼与被泼的畅快淋漓。同时，在景洪市的大街小巷，各傣家村寨特别是橄榄坝都有泼水活动。

注意事项：

泼水节期间的景洪市，早晚温差大，因此参加泼水活动时要做好衣服湿透的准备，带两套换洗衣服很有必要。参加泼水活动时最好不要随身携带手机或照相机等电子设备，除非它的防水性能足够好；尽量不要追逐打闹，不要去哄抢水源；不要使用脏水、污水参与泼水，文明泼水。

最佳旅游时间：

"热"是西双版纳气候的一大特色。西双版纳年平均气温21.9℃，分旱、雨两季。其中11-5月是旱季，天气凉爽，是旅游的旺季。尤其是在4月，这时候有盛大的泼水节。6-10月，是雨季，天气较湿热，但这个时间来版纳旅游能尝到各种水果。而且这时游人较少，各方面的花费也有所下降。

三
独具特色的民族竞技娱乐

泼水节期间，人们除了用泼水来表达祝福之外，还会举行放高升、放孔明灯、赛龙舟、选美、竹筏赛、射弩比赛、陀螺比赛、选果王和吃西瓜比赛等活动。通过竞技角逐，展现一个民族凝聚的力量，把民族最纯粹的性情及祈求表现得淋漓尽致。

放高升

高升是傣族人民自制的烟火。在当地人心目中，哪个村寨的高升飞得越高，哪个村寨就越光彩、越吉祥。所以，高升放得最高者会受到人们的赞赏。放高升比赛是智慧的较量。

新年的第一天，最主要的活动之一就是放高升，预示着新的一天的到来。高升，傣语叫作"莽斐"，是一种出现较早、较原始的火箭，使用竹筒装上火药而制成的。节日前夕，人们通常会在空旷的场地或者广场上用竹竿搭起数丈高的架子作为发射台。泼水节那天，将高升安放在竹架顶上，点燃后，"莽斐"会冒着白烟，拖着长长的尾巴飞向天空。随着"莽斐"的升起，穿着节日盛装的群众便会敲起铓锣，打起象脚鼓，跳起孔雀舞，唱起当地的民歌。随着高升升空的声音响彻天际，场面热闹动人。升得最高的"莽斐"的制作者会受到人们的钦佩和赞扬，也会得到一些物质上的奖励。

傣族制作高升的技艺非常高超。他们用几个竹筒装满木炭、硫磺、硝，做成火药筒。把火药筒捆绑在细长的竹竿上，安放在事先搭建好的竹架发射台上，点燃导火索之后，它便会冒着白烟冲向天空。高升分为单组、双组和多组等不同类型：只有一个火药筒绑在一根长竹竿上的称为单组；两个火药筒绑在一根长竹竿上就叫双组；多个火药筒便叫多组。单组、双组和多组的区分在于火药筒的数量，而作为高升一部分的长竹竿始终只有一根。当第一筒火药燃尽之后，第二筒的火药会开始燃烧，继续将高升推向高空，第二组燃尽后又会启动第三筒的火药，这样一来，高升会飞得更高。

放孔明灯

孔明灯又叫做"飞灯"，傣语叫"贡菲"，是西双版纳傣族创造的一种可以升空的"纸气球"。据传它是在佛教传入西双版纳后才发明的。当时，佛教信徒与民间宗教信仰者斗法，看谁做的东西飞得最高。民间宗教信仰者做了直射云霄的高升燃放，佛教弟子做了火飞灯燃放。当火红火红的纸灯笼飞上宁静的夜空时，场地上的人群一起仰头欢呼，大家一起载歌载舞以表示热烈，庆贺新年。孔明灯就是傣家人心目中的吉祥、快乐与自豪的象征。

赛龙舟

赛龙舟常常在泼水节的"麦帕雅晚玛"（第三天）举行。穿着节日盛装的群众欢聚在澜沧江畔、瑞丽江边和盈江沿岸观看龙舟竞渡。龙舟上画着精美的彩纹，坐着数名英武的划手，在木雕的龙尾上挂着一根饰有彩带的竹竿。比赛时，舟中间站立人击锣指挥，在规定的范围内，哪一队先到达目的地为胜。号令一响，整装待发的龙舟像箭一般往前飞去，顿时整条江面上鼓声、锣声、号子声、喝彩声此起彼伏，声声相应，节日的气氛在这里达到了高潮。龙舟比赛一般以一个村寨对另一个村寨进行。优胜的队伍会获得奖旗和奖品，同时也受到人们的祝贺和欢呼。人们趁着龙舟比赛结束之时的热闹场面，打起铜锣和象脚鼓，跳起傣族传统的舞蹈，以表示庆祝。

○澜沧江上赛龙舟

选美

泼水节选美是泼水节中最吸引人的活动之一。能够赢得最后比赛胜利的女孩一定是公认最才貌双全的。参加比赛的选手，一般要经过预选后才有资格进入最后的竞选。经过舞台走秀和才艺表演两个部分的激烈角逐，最终赢得观众最多掌声以及评委最亲睐的就是最后的"水姑娘"，意思是像水一样美丽的女孩。选美活动让泼水节增添了一道亮丽的风景线。

○参加选美的傣家少女（云南瑞丽）

射弩

弩是世界上最古老的兵器之一，是中国云、贵、川等地古代少数民族狩猎、打仗和防身用的一种工具。傣族的射弩比赛分为立姿和跪姿两个组别进行，均采取无依托立姿或跪姿发射。作为民族体育竞技项目出现在泼水节上，为泼水节增添了节日的气氛。

赛陀螺

陀螺是傣族民间流传深远的一项体育活动。它由当地文化部门牵头采取先报名后比赛的形式进行。比赛时由一个参赛者右手持带线竹棍，左手握住陀螺的中下方将线绕住陀螺，左手抛出陀螺，右手轻轻一拉，使陀螺着地旋转。比赛对手也用同样的方法，并且要击中旋转陀螺，在两个旋转的陀螺碰撞以后，仍在转动的为胜。

选果王

　　傣族生活的地区由于地理条件的优势，盛产西瓜、香蕉等水果。泼水节期间，每一个村寨会把本村最大的西瓜和最重的香蕉拿出来比赛，评选"西瓜王""香蕉王"，并以奖金的形式给予鼓励。凡是"各类王"的种植者还会被邀请到各村寨讲授种植的经验。

吃西瓜比赛

　　吃西瓜比赛是泼水节期间最刺激、最紧张的活动之一。为了让四方宾客感受傣乡魅力，泼水节组委会推出了吃西瓜比赛项目。西瓜盛宴是由参选西瓜王的各地西瓜组成。吃西瓜比赛没有男女之分，也没有名额限制，在规定的时间内吃完最多数量的参赛者为胜。"吃瓜王"们狼吞虎咽的吃像不时引来看客们阵阵的加油声和欢笑声，为泼水节活动增添了无限的乐趣。

四
有趣的"丢包"习俗

　　泼水节也是很多单身男女追求爱情、寻找对象的大好时节。每逢泼水节，青年男女都会异常高兴。对于"丢包"的期待从他们提前很多天忙于制作花包、挑选漂亮的衣服就可以窥视一二。泼水节前的 1 ～ 2 个星期，傣族姑娘便会开始准备缝制漂亮的花包，她们会挑选鲜艳的布料来缝制自己的花包。对于很多的单身年轻人来说，"丢包"可能是很容易的事情，就是丢与接的过程。但是，要亲手制作一个漂亮的花包会是一件难事。所以泼水节前夕，一些傣族少女会拿着她们挑选好的漂亮花布和针线，聚在一起向那些会制作花包的长辈们悉心学习制作的工艺。因为"丢包"是她们收获爱情的重要活动，所以她们也十分注重每一针一线的过程。从一针一线的缝制中可以看出傣族女孩性格中比较耐心、细心的一面，最终制作出来的花包也是很美的。

傣族姑娘和小伙们在泼水节当天挑选好美丽的服饰，准备一些礼物，打扮得漂漂亮亮的，约着去空旷的地方"丢包"。通常会分为男女两个方队，女的一边，男的在另一边，一男一女对丢。丢出的包如果一边接不住，就会被另外一边惩罚。惩罚的内容当然各不相同，很多是他们事先就想好的内容，也有一些惩罚项目是临时想出来的。通常小伙子若是接不到姑娘丢来的花包，就要把事先准备好的礼物送给姑娘，或者是将准备的鲜花戴在姑娘的头上；相反，若是姑娘接不住小伙子的花包，就得把鲜花戴在小伙子的胸前，将其当作送给小伙子的礼物。这样，从一来一往的丢包变成了交流的过程，一段段浪漫的爱情故事就这样开始了。

五

热情的舞蹈

歌舞相汇，歌声能悠扬婉转，抒情写意，舞蹈也不甘示弱。傣族人能歌善舞，多才多艺，泼水节期间自然少不了歌舞助兴。漂亮的盛装，雀跃的人群，流畅自如的肢体动作，承载着最自然的语言表达，借鉴孔雀的优美、雅致，效仿大象的稳健、踏实，伴着音乐，时而舒缓浪漫，时而明朗轻快，一颦一笑，一举一动，情感如行云流水，自然流露。

○泼水节中的傣家舞蹈（云南瑞丽）

孔雀舞

孔雀舞，傣语叫"嘎洛涌"。"洛涌"是孔雀的意思，"嘎"是跳舞的意思。孔雀舞是傣族最美丽的舞蹈之一，也是最受傣族人喜爱的舞蹈之一。富饶美丽的傣乡素有"孔雀之乡"的美称。过去，每当晨曦微明或夕阳斜照时，常见姿态旖旎的孔雀翩翩起舞，因此，孔雀在傣族人民心中是吉祥、幸福、美丽、善良的象征。每逢佳节，傣族人都要云集一堂，观看由民间艺人表演的根据民间故事、神话传说以及佛经故事等编成的孔雀舞及表现孔雀习性的舞蹈。比如，根据神话故事《魔鬼与孔雀》而编演的孔雀舞在民间广为流传。舞蹈表现了魔鬼欲霸占孔雀为妻，人面鸟身的孔雀奋力抖动自己美丽的羽毛，那绚丽、灿烂的光芒使魔鬼兄弟双目失明，孔雀取得了胜利。

孔雀舞还有另外一个美丽的传说。

相传在远古的时候，森林里住着一群快乐可爱、能歌善舞的孔雀精灵。只要他们一跳舞，整个森林便是一片欢腾。一天，不知从哪里来了两个恶魔，宣告这个森林是它们的领地，并且要求美丽的孔雀公主做它们的"王后"。孔雀公主假装高兴的样子，要恶魔到孔雀王国的宫殿与她成婚。她把恶魔引到了森林边的沼泽地里，恶魔很快被污泥吞没了，森林恢复了太平。孔雀公主唱歌跳舞，森林里又是一片欢乐。这只是流传于傣族中一则美丽动人的神话传说，傣家人将傣寨比喻成森林，而孔雀公主则是善良勇敢的化身，她们以智慧消灭了恶魔，拯救了整个森林。

孔雀舞是在盛大节日和"做摆"（修功德的佛会）时，在广场上表演的道具舞蹈。一般由 1～2 人或 3 人表演，但由于傣族分为不同的支系，孔雀在各地区的流传发展亦有不同，所以孔雀舞虽有较统一的表演程式，但也不是一个模式。傣族各地区的孔雀舞大同小

泼水节

异，技艺各有专长。西双版纳的孔雀舞至今仍保留着一雌一雄的孔雀双人舞，戴假面、挎孔雀架子，表演形式比较传统。瑞丽地区的孔雀舞以模仿孔雀的各种神态和动作为特点，有"飞跑下山""林中窥看""漫步森林""饮泉戏水""追逐嬉戏""展翅""拖翅""拌翅""点水"等造型优美的舞姿。其道具轻巧，技艺要求较高，民间艺人也比较多。芒市地区的孔雀舞多为碎步飞跑、原

○傣族孔雀舞

地转等以及手臂内屈和前轮翻腕的动作。舞者运用的碎步和手上动作为其他地区少有。以上的几种形式便是各地区傣族孔雀舞的形式、特点。它们之间的差别并不大，只是在一些细微末节中存在着差异。

孔雀舞风格浓郁，特点突出，感情内在而含蓄，舞姿富于雕塑感。以表现舞者的头部、手部、手指部、大臂部、小臂部、肘部、肩部、腰部、胯部、膝部等每一处身体的关节为主，肢体形态变化莫测，婀娜多姿。不论手的撩、推、拉、撤、晃，还是脚步的跳、挪、垫、跑、趾，孔雀舞中的美丽造型的舒展、流动表现出强烈鲜明的个性。不仅会使人们感到那秀丽山河的自然律动美，还会使人们感到傣族人心灵的平和与静谧、朴实与原始，更能使人感受到他们对美的理解和对甜蜜生活的向往。

傣族舞蹈中最具代表性和表现力的是杨丽萍的《雀之灵》，整个舞蹈将近 7 分钟，从舞蹈到开始到舞蹈结束，她所表现的那只孔雀，上身的造型和状态基本上是"三道弯"，也就是用腰部和胸部的前后

发力，通过上体三道弯和夸张地摆动胯部幅度展现出高枝欲飞的漂亮孔雀最原始、真实、自然、淳朴的基本造型。三道弯作为傣族舞蹈所特有的表现形式，主要展现出傣族女子如水般的柔美、细腻、温婉、可人、纤细、典雅的特色。

一顺边

"一顺边"的舞蹈姿态是从傣族所固有舒展的、平静的基本舞姿动律中提炼出来的，主要呈现出一些祥和与安逸、渴望与美好的舞蹈意向。虽然傣族大多生活在坝子中，但高原山地的地域形态直接映射在当地人民日常劳动的步态和形体动态中。山路崎岖，人们往来间有诸多不便，上山、下坡自不必说，就是一般走路也和在平原上大有不同，其主要区别，就在于脚掌的着力点和身体的平衡上，于是逐渐形成了"一顺边"的体态。

象脚鼓

象脚鼓是泼水节中最为重要的舞蹈乐器之一。傣族象脚鼓分长象脚鼓、中象脚鼓、小象脚鼓三种。长象脚鼓舞蹈动作不多，以打法变化、鼓点丰富见长。有一指打、二指打、三指打、掌打、拳打、肘打、脚打、头打等。多为一人表演，或为舞蹈伴奏。长象脚鼓是象脚鼓中最高大的一种，傣语称"光亚"，一般在 130～160 厘米，最高的达 190 厘米，鼓面直径 30 厘米左右。中象脚鼓一般用拳打，个别地区用槌打。没有更多鼓点，一般一拍打一下，个别地区左手指加打弱拍。以鼓音长短、音色高低及舞蹈时鼓尾摆动大小为标准。据说鼓音长者，可打一槌鼓将衣服钮扣全部解开，再一槌鼓将钮扣全部扣好，鼓音仍不完。中象脚鼓舞步扎实稳重刚健，大动作及大舞姿较多。舞蹈时不限定人数，人少时对打，人多时围成圆圈打。中鼓，傣语称"光吞"，是象脚鼓中用途最广的一种。鼓高 60 ～ 95 厘米，鼓面直径 23 ～ 28 厘米，鼓底直径 23 ～ 31 厘米。中腰最细处直径 11 ～ 15 厘米，常用于象脚鼓舞或节日庆祝。小象脚鼓仅在西双版纳多见，舞步灵活跳跃，以斗鼓、赛鼓为特点。斗和赛中有灵活、机智的进攻、退让，以最后抓住对方帽子或包头为胜。一般为二人对赛。小鼓外形有如矮脚杯状，高仅 30 ～ 40 厘米，应用不如大、中型鼓广泛。

象脚鼓舞

象脚鼓舞在泼水节中扮演着重要的角色。西双版纳的男子，从青少年到年老者都会跳象脚鼓舞。一般来说，由一个男子边击鼓边领跳，其他人陆续加入舞队，踏着有力的鼓点，抬脚起舞，有的象脚鼓舞还要边唱边跳。舞队逐渐壮大，每到高潮时，场面热烈，气势磅礴，十分壮观。跳象脚鼓舞的男子，身挎两头蒙着牛皮、形状似象脚的长鼓。鼓的腰间系上彩带或者花布，斜挎在舞者的肩上，边击鼓，边跳舞。随着热烈欢快的节奏，脚步踏地有力，双膝曲直交替，身体上下起伏，宛如漫步在丛林中的大象，其步伐稳健有力，舞姿洒脱自如。

○我的泼水节（云南景洪）

西双版纳傣族歌舞表演

初到西双版纳的,可以去体验一下西双版纳精彩的歌舞表演。泼水节期间,孔雀舞和象脚鼓舞都会在节日期间进行演出。若是平日里来到西双版纳,在曼听公园、西双版纳傣族园或勐巴拉娜西艺术宫等景点也能欣赏到热情的民族舞蹈,其中较为著名的是《澜沧江·湄公河之夜》《勐巴拉娜西》等大型歌舞表演。

六
独特的傣家服饰

每到泼水节,傣族男女老少都会穿上节日盛装,载歌载舞,相互泼水祝福。傣族小伙朴实大方,头缠布巾,挎上背带,一袭小短袖衫配搭净色宽腰无兜长裤。傣族姑娘短衣贴身,筒裙艳丽,举手抬足婀娜多姿,洒脱轻逸。

傣族女子服饰

傣族聚居地属亚热带雨林气候的坝区，天气炎热，雨量充沛，植物繁茂，湖泊交错和河川纵横。生活在此的傣族人身材纤细，体形较小，属于娇小玲珑型。生活中傣族姑娘喜欢穿着窄袖短衣和花筒裙，这种筒裙长及脚踝，高齐腰，紧紧裹着下身，充分展示了女性的胸、腰、臀"三围"流线之美，加上所采用的布料轻柔、鲜艳、明快，不仅能凸现女性的妩媚，还给人一种婀娜多姿、潇洒飘逸的感觉。女性的服饰，各地差异较大，但几乎所有的傣族都穿着筒裙。筒裙，又作"桶裙"或"统裙"，因无褶皱、裙身形似圆桶而得名。提及筒裙，人们自然会想到傣族姑娘身着筒裙婀娜俏丽的倩影，筒裙因此也成了傣族的标志之一。

不同地区傣族女性的服饰有所差异。

西双版纳傣族妇女的传统服饰为上着黑色长袖右衽圆领紧身短衣，襟边镶有数道彩条，下身为从上腰处长及脚背的黑色裹身筒裙，用银腰带束紧，裙上部织以暗红色为主的彩条。现代女性的服饰则色彩艳丽，款式多样，有吊带式、圆领式等。发式不论老幼皆盘发髻于脑后，或松散偏于后脑右上端，饰以小巧发梳或发簪等饰物。从服饰上看，西双版纳傣族的服饰更富于创新性，色彩艳丽。

金平傣族妇女的传统服饰为上着白色对襟齐腰长袖紧身衣，老年妇女也有穿蓝色或浅蓝色的；下着长及脚背的黑色筒裙，裙边多嵌以彩色花边；腰间系一条绿色或绯红色的绸质腰带；扣子为蝴蝶形银质排扣，这是该族群独具特色的服饰特点。长衣为黑色，类似风衣，多为老年妇女穿着。现代服饰无太大变化，基本保留了传统的款式和色彩。从整体看，金平傣族的服饰款式倾于传统，色彩典雅，以黑、白为主，其他色彩多做点缀。

○ "走，泼水去"（云南芒市）

傣族男子服饰

　　在现今的日常生活、劳动和节日中，女子还会穿着傣族传统的服饰，但傣族男子的服饰已经发生了重大变化。无论是在金平还是在德宏、西双版纳等傣族地区，傣族男子的服饰基本上和汉族的穿衣打扮没有太大的差别了，只是在泼水节等重要的节日和重要的场合才会穿着傣族传统服饰。但是在过去，傣族男子的服饰反映了他们居住在水边的这一生态特色。男子会用白色或淡蓝色的布来包头，通常穿白色或者黑色的衬衣和裤筒比较宽的筒裤。衬衫和裤子的颜色常常是一样的，还会在衣服的边角处用金色的线绣上一些图案、花边。傣族男子的服装色彩一般比较淡雅，稍显暗淡。男子的裤筒较宽与他们常常接触水、河流有关系，在过河时很容易就能够把裤子往上卷，而且可以卷得很高，泼水节时被祝福的圣水泼湿了以后能快速变干。

文身

　　古代文献中，凡是提到傣族先民的，无一不会提到他们文身的习俗。文身是傣族最具有特色的身体装饰，也是傣族的重要标志之

一。在很久前，这种装饰身体的习俗，傣族男子必须是人人都要有的，否则会遭到社会的排斥。《百夷传》说："百夷，其首皆髡，胫皆黥，不髡者杀之，不黥者众叱笑，比之妇女。"

文身一般多见于男子，女子文身者很少，即使文也多在手腕或者在臂部刺一些简单的图案，或刺自己的名字，亦有佛经文。文身并没有严格的年龄限制，但通常是在 12 ~ 30 周岁之间。文身的部位也没有严格限定，身体的各个部位都可以。傣族古代文身分等级，可以用文身来区分身份地位的高低。《西南夷风土记》记载："男子皆黥其下体成文，以别贵贱，部夷黥至腿，目把黥至腰，土官黥至乳。"贵族可以选择刺红色纹样，普通百姓就只能刺黑色或是青黑色的花纹。文身的花纹有动物形状，多为老虎、狮子、大象、龙、孔雀、鸟、蛇等；有文字、简单的佛经、人名、佛名等；也有线条、花纹、水波纹、直线、圆圈等。

文身的方法一般有两种。一种是用针或者刀片之类锋利的器物在肌肤上刺或者刻画出各种想要的图案，然后涂上颜料；另一种是在针头上缠一些线或者纱布，把针头露出来，蘸着颜料和墨汁直接在肌肤上刺。纱布上的颜料干了又蘸，一直到刺成一个完整的图案。

在傣族人看来，文身不仅仅是重要的装饰和体面的标志，更重要的一点是，在他们的宗教观念当中文身还可以防鬼怪、驱邪避害。男子文身之后就会变得更加勇敢和担当，会变成有魅力的男人。

饰齿

饰齿分染齿和镶齿，都是借助其他物质来改变牙齿颜色的一种方式。西双版纳和金平傣族的染齿大同小异，一般有两种方法：一种是将栗木用火熏出烟来，把烟烘烤在小铁片上，用手蘸着烟汁染齿；另一种是通过长期嚼食植物使牙齿由红变黑，经久不褪。此种方法在两地不尽相同，金平傣族是嚼食一种当地称为"部"的藤叶植物，嚼时搀入草烟、石灰等物。西双版纳一带的傣族，则多以嚼食槟榔为主。镶齿即用金属片做成牙套镶嵌在门牙上，成为"金齿"或"银齿"。男女均有镶齿习俗，而染齿则多在已婚的妇女当中。

七

可口的傣家美食

　　傣族饮食文化经历了悠久的历史，在中国的美食长廊中有着重要的地位，既有适应生态环境的特征，又有人文精神的特征，并以其鲜明的饮食文化在中国的美食界广受欢迎。傣味不仅在傣族地区

○泼水节中的盛宴（云南耿马）

受到人们的亲睐,在一些城市也有很多喜欢傣味的人群。泼水节来临,傣家人便忙着杀猪、宰鸡、酿酒、准备烧烤食材,还要做许多"毫诺索"(年糕),用糯米做成多种粑粑,采摘各种新鲜水果和野菜,以供节日里食用。傣族传统饮食文化具有鲜明的特征。

突出酸和辣

傣族喜食酸和辣,这与傣族居住地气候炎热、空气潮湿有很大的关系。气候的炎热往往会影响人们的食欲,酸不仅能提神、开胃、助消化,还能去腥味。带酸味的食物在炎热的地方不易变质,所以酸笋煮鸡、酸笋煮鱼、酸笋煮牛干巴、柠檬凉拌鸡等菜都是以酸为美、以酸取胜的傣味佳肴。吃辣可以除湿,减少风湿病的痛楚,傣族尤其喜欢用新鲜的小米辣做菜,傣味烧烤、包烧、蘸水都不能没有辣,可以说,没有辣就不是傣味,甚至傣味有"无辣不成菜"之说。

喜爱糯食

傣族是中国种植水稻最早的民族之一。各地傣族均以食用稻米为主,糯米是傣族的主食。糯米饭冷热都好吃,为了抓紧时间做活,傣家人下地劳动时,常常带糯米饭作为中餐。农忙时节,傣族妇女会早早起来,把前一天晚上泡好的糯米蒸好,用芭蕉叶包住(有的是装在竹篾编成的饭盒里)后放进竹篮里,带上一些腌菜、酱、油炸牛肉干等就出工了。中午,坐在田间地头就开饭了。糯米黏黏的,有弹性,不仅香软可口还耐食,有嚼劲、不易饿、不油腻、不易掉落。所以糯米饭备受傣家人的亲睐。傣族人认为:吃糯米饭能使姑娘身材苗条,小伙子则善跳能跑。

糯米不仅是傣族平常生活的主食,也是制作一系列辅食的重要食材。如"毫糯索""毫崩""毫焖""毫邦""毫邦噜"等都是最常见的糯米制品。每逢傣历新年，傣族家家户户都要做许多这类食品，自己吃或卖或送亲朋好友。毫糯索相当于汉族的年糕。傣家人说："吃了毫糯索，人就长了一岁。"更有菠萝糯米饭，又香又甜，被称为傣族饮食的一绝。竹筒饭也是傣族比较喜欢的美食，把泡过的糯米放在竹筒里蒸煮，煮出来的饭不仅保持了原有的糯米香味，还有了竹子的清香。

腌菜和酱料丰富

傣族人喜欢吃腌菜，也擅长做腌菜。腌菜的种类多种多样，不仅有腌蔬菜，如腌萝卜、腌白菜等，也有腌猪肉、腌牛肉、腌鱼等。这些腌菜既酸又辣，特别符合傣族人的口味。吃饭的时候，用小碗装一些腌菜直接作菜，或把腌菜作为配料与其他菜一起煮着吃，酸辣的味道既开胃又下饭。酱，傣语称为"喃咪"。在傣族餐桌上，可以没有肉食，但不可没喃咪。傣族喃咪品种多样，不同的蔬菜蘸不同的喃咪，包括"喃咪布"（螃蟹酱）、"喃咪帕"（蔬菜酱）、"喃咪麻黑松"（番茄酱）、"喃咪偌"（竹笋酱）、"喃咪麻批"（辣子酱）、"喃咪巴"（鱼酱）、"喃咪托领"（花生酱）、"喃咪麻个"（嘎哩啰酱），等等。傣族赞哈唱道："吃饭没有喃咪，就像生活中没有爱情，日子都没有味道。"可见，喃咪在傣族饮食文化中占有重要地位。

偏爱野菜和素菜

在寻找能食用的野菜方面，傣族是一个勇于探索和敢于尝试的民族。他们会用传统的方式去发现各种各样的野菜，经过很多人的试吃，为后代留下宝贵的经验。经过祖辈们留下的经验和年轻一代的不断探索，傣族人认识了许多可以食用的山茅野菜，叫得出名的就有90多种。

青苔，是傣族食品中的天然"绿藻"。从河里捞来，摊成薄饼后晒干，可以油煎，也可揉碎用葱花、油盐炒。吃糯米饭时，抓一小撮夹在饭中间，色泽鲜绿，口感清香细腻，让人食欲大增。

杂菜，是傣族人喜欢的又一道家常菜。把几种蔬菜混杂在一起煮汤，据说这样做，一顿饭就可以吃到好几

○ 遮放泼水节中的美食（云南芒市）

种菜，营养丰富。通常合在一起煮的菜有：小米菜、南瓜尖、小白菜、甜菜叶，再加少许臭菜、小米辣和生姜丝等。煮菜只放盐不放油，汤色澄清碧绿，各种植物芳香汇在一起，形成独特的味道。

傣族喜欢在自家庭院的围墙边种扁豆、四棱豆。新鲜的豆荚摘来用清水煮熟，捞在碗里，做一个花生酱，一道味道天然的佳肴就做好了。另外，水香菜、莲花白、茴香、薄荷、刺五加、野茄子、黄瓜、鱼腥草等都是傣家蘸酱生吃的蔬菜。烧烤的茄子、韭菜等，与蘸酱配着吃，味道很独特。傣族喜欢素食，一方面得益于他们的制作方法极大地保留了植物的清香味和维生素等营养；另一方面，酱酸辣有味，在气候湿热的傣族地区，这种清爽味重的素食最为适宜。所以，除了节庆，傣族平时以素食为主。与汉族比较，傣族食用蔬菜主要是做法不同。汉族对蔬菜的烹饪方法主要是煮、炒；傣族更多是生吃或开水烫熟后捞起蘸酱吃。与大油爆炒相比，傣族做法更清新爽口。

烹饪方式多样

傣族饮食文化的一个重要特征是多样的烹饪技术。烹饪技术有烧、烤、蒸、剁、腌、舂、炸、煎、煮、拌，等等。

"烧烤"是傣族烹饪文化中最常见的烹饪技艺之一。傣族食肉喜欢烧烤，用"烤"的方法烹制的菜肴有香茅草烤鱼、香茅草烤鸡、烤猪肉、烤牛干巴等。烧烤时选料要精细，还要加入众多的配料及调料，火候也要掌握好，使肉黄而不焦，外脆里嫩。

包烧也是傣味中常用的烹饪技艺。傣族人先把要烧的菜用各种调料调好味道，再用芭蕉叶把调好味的菜包在里面，用两个铁架夹住，在火炭上翻动烘烤。待芭蕉叶烧到焦黑时，里面的菜就熟了。用包烧的方式做出来的菜香嫩可口。一方面，芭蕉叶锁住了菜中原有的水分，保持了菜鲜嫩；另一方面，包烧是在火炭上隔着芭蕉叶的烧烤，也具有了烧烤和芭蕉叶的香味。包烧的主要菜式有包烧猪肉、包烧牛肉、包烧鱼、包烧各种蔬菜等。与包烧不同，在德宏的傣族中还有一道节日期间家家户户必食、极富特色的火烧肉米线。制作时，将猪腹部的五花肉切成大块的薄片，用盐、酒、味精、辣椒、酱油、香料等进行腌制，然后把肉穿在铁钎上置于大火上烧。烧到肉熟之后拿下来切碎，再放入豌豆粉和米线，加上盐、味精、芫荽、蒜泥、酱油、辣椒油、芝麻油、花生末等调味料，最重要的是要放上傣家特别熬制的"酸水"，然后搅拌均匀即可实用。

炸的菜肴主要有油炸竹虫、油炸鱼、油炸猪皮、油炸青苔、油炸年糕等。煎的菜肴主要有青苔煎鸡蛋、青椒煎鸡蛋、煎牛肉片等。油炸和煎的区别在于，前者是在盛有很多油的锅里完成，而煎通常不需要太多的油。油炸和煎所用的油通常是菜籽油，因为菜籽油煎炸出来的食品更好看。

傣族有木制的蒸锅，也有铁制的蒸锅。木蒸锅用来蒸米饭，铁

多彩中国节

泼水节

蒸锅用来蒸菜。因为用蒸的方式做出来的饭和菜具有鲜、嫩、香的特点，吃了不上火，男女老幼皆宜。傣族人将热带水果中的菠萝和米饭一起蒸，做出来的"菠萝饭"很受欢迎。菠萝的味道甜蜜、适合开胃，菠萝饭营养丰富、制作简单，成了很受傣族人和其他民族游客青睐的主食。除了蒸米饭外，用蒸的方式做的菜肴主要有蒸火腿、蒸香肠、蒸牛干巴、蒸鱼、蒸鸡蛋等，主要是蒸一些晒干后容易上火的荤菜。

○傣家菠萝饭（云南盈江）

用"煮"的方法烹调的菜肴有青菜、酸笋鸡、酸笋鱼、田螺、牛扒呼等。傣族喜欢吃酸，在煮食中都要加入酸笋、西红柿或者酸水果（酸木瓜、酸茄）。如煮青菜，特别是苦青菜，傣语叫"酸耙菜"，青菜洗净不切，用手拧断成4～5厘米长的菜段，放入沸水中煮，同时放上少许姜丝和一个西红柿或者是酸笋和其他的酸果子，不放油盐。菜熟后配着调好的蘸水蘸着吃，味道清淡但是很开胃。

剁生通常选用新鲜牛肉或猪肉等，经过舂黏或剁细后制成。分为三种：一种是拌佐料吃；一种是剁细不煮熟吃；一种是剁细了煮熟吃。用"剁"的方法烹调的菜肴有猪肉剁生、牛肉剁生、鱼肉剁生、麂子肉剁生等。在傣族看来，凡是肉类，都可以做剁生。"剁生"是傣族的下酒名菜，具有香甜可口、味道酸辣的特点。

腌则分为熟腌和生腌两种。用"腌"的方法烹调的菜肴有腌牛脚筋、腌黄牛皮、腌猪脚、腌鱼、腌笋丝、腌酸菜、腌蕨菜等几十种。在傣族等民族中较常见的"酸水"，就是就餐时使用的传统蘸水，是用"腌"的方式制作而成的。制作方法为：腊月间，将萝卜连根拔起、晒干，用熬好的糯米稀饭加水泡制，每日翻搅，直至发酸。然后将酸水舀出放入锅中熬制、收浓即成"酸水"。腌过的萝卜菜仍然可以放入锅里的酸水中熬，熬好晾干，即成"干腌菜"，可做酸汤用。用不完的"酸水"继续熬，熬制浓稠成为膏状，成为"腌菜膏"。平日里没有"酸水"的时候拿出来用水调开，拌凉拌菜用。这样的"酸水"，一年四季皆可食。

用"舂"的方法烹调的菜肴有各种喃咪酱。如螃蟹酱就是将螃蟹肉舂细，放在锅里用水熬，熬到浓汁呈厚膏状为止，取出晒干备用。吃时，将青辣椒、蒜、葱等佐料切细放在碗里，取一块螃蟹干片放在一起，加入适量开水和盐，用舂盐棒研细，即可用糯米饭蘸着吃，味道辛辣清香。另外，把茄子、番茄烧烤后去皮拌上葱、姜、蒜、芫荽、辣椒、盐等佐料舂成泥状，也是傣族家常吃法。现代家庭多用电器，不便烧烤，就把茄子、番茄或蒸或煮熟后，去皮加入各种佐料舂细，味道也不错。

凉拌的主要菜肴有柠檬鸡、柠檬撒、苦撒、凉拌黄瓜、凉拌猪皮、凉拌鱼腥草等。"柠檬鸡"是傣味里面最受欢迎的菜之一，柠檬的香和酸味，配上小米辣的辣味，让柠檬鸡成了最开胃提神的荤菜。"牛撒撇"也是傣族最具特色的菜式之一，"牛撒撇"有两种，分别为"酸撒"和"苦撒"。两者的区别在于一个是酸辣味的，一个是苦辣味的。"苦撒"不用柠檬，用的是牛胃里的苦水。牛宰杀后，把牛胃里面的东西用纱布过滤出液体来，再将液体拿到锅里煮沸（目的是为了杀菌），变凉之后就可以拿去拌"苦撒"了。

自酿米酒

酒不仅是散湿气、御风寒、解疲劳的饮料，还是傣族招待客人的佳品。在傣族心中，无酒不成宴，只要有酒，哪怕是吃酸腌菜，他们也高兴。傣族人爱喝自己酿的米酒，他们会把酿好的米酒放在陶罐里，放置在阴凉的地方，等待节日来临的时候，宴请亲朋好友来品尝美食美酒。他们以酒迎客，以酒伴歌舞，以酒加深友情。

新鲜的水果

傣族居住的地区多为热带或者亚热带，所以产的水果多为热带水果，如芒果、椰子、榴莲、荔枝、甘蔗、菠萝蜜等。泼水节来临时正是西瓜、香蕉、菠萝成熟的季节。在临沧市永德县永康镇勐底傣族村，泼水节的前一天或两天，村长会带着几个村民，开着拖拉机到村民的田地里去收西瓜或者香蕉。村长召集村民开会，说泼水节就要来了，我们需要每家每户捐几个西瓜、几斤香蕉来欢迎参加我们泼水节的远方客人。然后约定一个时间，村长便会带着村民到每家每户的西瓜田里收西瓜，去香蕉田里收香蕉。通常，收到的都是村民们自己挑出来个头大的瓜果，村民们愿意捐出更好的瓜果是为了让来参与他们节日的朋友能够感受到他们的心意。村长开着装满各种水果的拖拉机回到村中寺庙，并把这些水果放到寺庙里，等到泼水节那一天拿出来免费给外来的游客和本村的村民品尝。泼水节那天，西瓜连着皮被切成一片一片的放在干净的盘子里，香蕉也是放在盘子里，所有的水果都会摆放在寺庙的阴凉处，人们泼水泼累了的时候就会跑到那里去品尝这些美味水果。

○泼水节中的水果（云南盈江）

美味的"粑粑"

粑粑是云南各民族非常喜爱的日常食品。傣族等民族的粑粑在制作技艺、食用方法、用途上有所差异。泼水节临近的前一两周，傣族妇女会赶着做很多的"粑粑"，有"芭蕉叶粑粑""糯米粑粑""风吹粑粑""糯米粒粑粑"等。这些"粑粑"除了需要在泼水节那天拿到寺庙里面去"赕佛"（即供奉给佛祖）外，也供全家食用。傣族人喜欢吃糯米饭，自然也就喜欢用糯米做出来的各种点心。每年的泼水节，傣族人都会做很多这样的糯米点心，一方面是他们食用的需求量大，另一方面是在参与泼水节中的其他民族中，这些傣族的"粑粑"也很受欢迎。一些妇女会在泼水节这一天，在寺庙旁边或者在集市里做起卖这些"粑粑"的生意。游客来傣族村寨体验泼水乐趣的同时会去品尝傣家的美味食物，也有人会把这些食物带回去给家人品尝。每一年的泼水节，卖"傣族粑粑"妇女都会获得一笔比较可观的收入。

"毫焖"是傣语，意思就是芭蕉叶粑粑，顾名思义就是用芭蕉叶包起来的糯米粑粑。制作时需要的原料和材料有嫩绿的芭蕉叶、白糯米、红糖、纱布、石磨等。先把淘洗干净的糯米用清水侵泡3个小时左右，再把泡好的生糯米用石磨碾磨成细细的米粉。现在，随着科技的发展，手工磨米的传统已经渐渐被磨米机取代了。碾磨出来的是带水的生米粉，所以要用纱布将水沥干，之后将沥干的米粉放在盆里和碾碎的红糖搅拌均匀。红糖的量根据人们的口味和喜好来加。最后就是取适量带糖的生米粉用芭蕉叶包成长方体的形状，放入蒸锅里蒸2个小时，出炉后尝到的便是热腾腾的、充满芭蕉叶香、红糖香、糯米香的傣族芭蕉叶粑粑了。芭蕉叶粑粑广受傣族人民的欢迎，不仅因为其味道香甜可口，还因为这种粑粑冷热都能吃，不需要重新加工，其本身就有红糖，也不需要再去蘸其他的东西了。

"毫崩"就是糯米粑粑的意思，傣族人会在泼水节或者春节期间舂这种糯米粑粑。与芭蕉叶粑粑不同的是，糯米粑粑是用蒸熟了的糯米舂碎以后粘在芭蕉叶或者是平整的塑料薄膜上，晾干、变凉以后用火炭烘烤着吃，一般会用芝麻、蜂蜜、白糖、红糖等蘸着吃。

"风吹粑粑"之所以有此称谓，傣族人说是因为这种粑粑很薄、很轻，用嘴一咬就会碎，会化在嘴里；人们吃了就会身轻如燕，会感觉到像一阵风吹过，加上泼水节期间会起大风，傣家人称这段时间的风为"新年大风"，而食用的这种粑粑就被叫做"风吹粑粑"了。

"米粒粑粑"是直接将蒸熟的糯米饭轻轻地摁成直径为5厘米左右的小圆饼，再拿到干净的席子上，放在太阳下面晒干了以后浸泡在熬好的糖水中，又取出来晒干，最后把晒干的粑粑用油炸成金黄色。油炸出来的"米粒粑粑"香脆甜美，外表呈现出的是一粒一粒的糯米饼，故谓之"米粒粑粑"。

　　傣族饵丝是德宏傣族的传统食品，节日期间必不可少。制作饵丝时，将米磨细、煮熟、再磨，可用糯米也可以用一般的米做。只不过最后要用碾饵丝的机器碾成大片，然后卷起来成一卷。吃时再把一卷饵丝一刀刀横切开，宽度大概在5厘米左右，全部抖开就成丝状了。下锅煮过之后放到事先备好的肉汤里，加上调味料就可以吃了。不过供斋的饵丝是不放油的，只放开水和一点红糖。

八
本真的"赶摆"

　　商贸集市是城乡民众休闲、娱乐、消费集中的地方。泼水节中的商贸集市无处不彰显着一个民族本真和独特的文化。"赶摆"是傣族节日的统称，又称"做摆"。其实，傣族人"赶摆"的涵盖面，远比集市贸易要宽泛得多，是集祭祀、集会、百艺、商贸于一体的民间聚会。傣族的节日尽管名目繁多，却大都叫做"摆"，如摆爽南（泼水节）、摆干朵、摆帕拉、摆拉罗、摆汗尚、摆奘、摆斋等，参加这些活动，都叫做赶摆。

　　1940年，人类学家田汝康到云南芒市那目寨进行了10个月的田野调查工作，他在其《芒市边民的摆》中写道："摆是一种宗教仪式，但是这个仪式却关联着摆夷（傣族）的整个生活，它如同维摩诘经中所谓的须弥、芥子一样，在一个小小的宗教仪式中，竟容纳了整个摆夷文化的全面影响，甚而还启示我们对现时许多经济、社会、政治问题产生一种新的看法。"在这本著作中，田汝康先生对傣族每个不同阶段年龄的人的佛教崇拜仪式、"摆"的类型和仪式过程进行了介绍。随着时间的流逝，赶摆发生了一些变化，但是赶摆仍然是泼水节中最具特色的风景线。

到了赶摆的时候，村寨里的群众一齐汇集到佛寺内诵经，男人们击鼓敲锣，迎请佛像。待佛像一到，身着盛装的女人们立刻献花、供果，焚香燃烛。节日里，人们还常常唱傣戏或做其他表演，开展娱乐活动。未婚的青年男女趁此机会互相求爱，寻找意中人。当日，"做摆"的主人还要请众人宴饮。按照传统习惯，自己做了一次摆，在宗教上的地位就升为"坦"，二次升为"帕嘎"，三次升为"帕戛勒"，四次升为"帕戛勒相"。地位越高，越得到村人的尊敬，所以民间做摆的习俗一直延续下来。

俗话说："谷子黄，傣家狂。"此时正是稻谷金黄，丰收在望的季节，也是"摆干朵"最热闹的时节。"摆干朵"的时间长短，因地而异，根据各地有影响的较大奘房而定。一般是一个奘房赶一个摆，如芒市较大的奘房有风平、尖山、广母、芒幸、奘相、奘茂、奘喊等七处，所以芒市的"摆"就得七天。而瑞丽、盈江、陇川、梁河等地则赶摆3～5天。摆场设在奘房附近比较宽阔的地方，食品、货摊、驰名省内外的阿昌刀、户撒和弄岛毛烟等，比比皆是，琳琅满目。还有傣家独具一格的筒帕、银手饰、软耳丝等。

赶摆时，人们穿着节日盛装，高抬供品。浩浩荡荡的队伍，拥向摆场。那鲜艳夺目的服装，摆曳的花筒裙，还有正在热恋的伴侣，拥向人群，围观孔雀舞，看傣族戏。进入集市首先看到的是傣族妇女们忙碌的身影，用传统的扁担挑着小竹篓。站在高处看：老人进奘房烧香拜佛，求子求孙求发财，祈求佛祖保佑平安；中年人正在进行象脚鼓比赛，跳孔雀舞，演傣戏；青年男女在花伞下，窃窃私语，有的干脆跑到野外，谈情说爱去了。只见一把把花伞向竹林深处移动，无声地宣告一天的赶摆结束。第二天，又要赶到其他摆场看热闹了。

泼水节会场附近的赶摆集市一般经营小吃，如酸笋煮鱼、酸笋煮牛干巴、柠檬凉拌鸡、糯米粑粑、烧烤和各种新鲜水果等，也有民族服饰、家禽、土特产品，外来商户则经营服饰、鞋帽、文具、玩具、音像制品、电子产品以及生产工具、农副产品、蔬菜、水果等，甚至还有各种娱乐项目。大大小小的摊位、形形色色的商品、八方商贾云集、游客你来我往，整个场面甚是热闹。

由于泼水节的广泛传播，慕名前来的外地游客、学者、摄影者越来越多。泼水节的集市，不仅满足了人们商品交易和消费的需求，更重要的是承载了文化交流的功能，成为多种文化流动的空间。在赶摆的集市上能充分领略到当地少数民族的多样化风俗，包括衣俗、食俗、礼俗、艺俗等，赶摆成为了一个浓缩的民族文化集市。

旅游小贴士

西双版纳"赶摆"

赶摆是傣族的一种传统活动，赶摆的内容实际上比集市贸易要宽泛得多。西双版纳最大的赶摆场位于景洪市告庄西双景赶摆街，汇集了东南亚民间文化及艺人、各地特色小吃、工艺品、土特产等。此外，泼水节期间澜沧江边和曼听公园也会举行赶摆，澜沧江赶摆是在裸露的河滩上进行；曼听公园的赶摆活动则以逛公园、观看舞蹈表演为主。

注意事项：

西双版纳天气炎热，一定要带上足够多的 T 恤和短裤，最好带一件薄外套。此外，参加赶摆时太阳镜、防晒霜、遮阳帽、防中暑药（例如霍香正气胶囊）都必不可少。

最佳旅游时间：

每年11-5月是旱季，天气凉爽，是旅游的旺季。尤其是在4月，这时候有盛大的泼水节，赶摆规模尤为盛大。

○赶摆路上歇歇脚（云南孟连）

Chapter Two
The Customs of the Water-Splashing Festival

Traditional ethnic festivals are gradually formed by all ethnic groups in order to adapt to the production practice and social life in the course of history. They are a collection of culture matters of folk customs, economic and trade activities, recreation and sports, and reflect in different degree the social history, religious belief, life style and psychological quality of the ethnic groups.

"Water-Splashing Festival" is the "living fossil" of the traditional culture of Dai and other ethnic groups. The myths, legends, folk beliefs, traditional costumes, beautiful dances and rural markets are preserved in the festival activities. The "Water-Splashing Festival" not only reflects the religious beliefs and good wishes of the ethnic groups, but also is a great display of religious culture, costume culture, food culture, marriage culture, culture of dances and songs, and entertainment culture.

During the festival, water mist diffuses, and every ethnic person is dressed in festival costumes and immersed in the atmosphere of blessings. They splash water on each other, and the filed is full of crowding people, happiness, laughter, music, and colorful flags. Each splashing water is like a happy smiling face, with high enthusiasm and blessings. The more water is splashed, the higher the voice of blessings will be. Love is hopeful, the strength recovered, the dancing alive, the fireworks flickering, and every year is better than the last. Every drop of water, infused with the infinite sincerity, is sprinkled to the world as the blessing of peace, health and good luck, and delivers the most original and purest friendship blessings.

Speaking of the Water–Splashing Festival, the first thing in mind is Dai nationality. This festival is not only the most solemn festival of Dai nationality, but also one of the most popular and most participated festivals in ethnic festivals of Yunnan Province. Today, the ritual and content of the festival have changed a lot, but the core functions of blessing and entertainment have been preserved.

1.The Sacred Religious Beliefs

The Dai nationality is one with a long history and splendid culture, which has not only their own language, but also their own writing. Pali Language Buddhism they believe in is national, so the Buddhist architecture is spread throughout Dai villages. The Buddhist temples and pagodas are elegant and delicate, which fully reflect the religious beliefs of Dai people. Moreover, the brilliant literature and art provide the mural painting of Buddhist temples with excellent writing materials, and Jinghong enjoys the fame of "the world of line modeling beauty". When creating the Buddhist temple murals, Dai people are good at originality, and also adept at absorbing and immitating other nations' excellent art. They make lines with feelings and express feelings with lines, and absorb the strengths of others to enrich themselves, which makes the mural art of Buddhist temples more colorful and become an exotic flower

Flying water (Mangshi, Yunnan Province)

among Dai people's art treasure house. During the festival, people express their piety and determination to Buddhism through such activities as bathing the Buddha, chanting sutras, and piling up sand.

Bathing the Buddha is one of the symbols most representing the ritual respect of people who believe in the Southern Sect of Buddhism.

"Bathing the Buddha" is to wash the Buddha statue with water, including the meaning of baptism. Dai people yearn for the Buddha, respect the Buddha and worship the Buddha, and behave themselves in the spirit of benevolence and kindness. And the Buddha, in the heart of Dai people, is always so solemn, so holy, and so benevolent. Why should the Buddha statue be bathed? It turns out to be that, to the pious Dai people, even if the supreme Buddha with boundless power is vulnerable sometime to the vulgar world, so mortals are needed to help wash away from the Buddha statue the dust and dirt contaminated in the world every year. Therefore, Dai people will hold a grand "bathing the Buddha" ceremony during every Dai New Year.

The Dai New Year usually lasts three days. The first day is called "Wanmai", on which all the families should clean up, unpick and clean the bedding, and welcome the New Year neatly. The second day is called "Wannao", which is an empty day, namely, it is counted neither in the Old Year nor in the New Year. The third day, called "Maipayawanma" in Dai language, is the day when "King of days" comes to the world. This day is the start of "bathing the Buddha" ceremony and the grand "Water-Splashing Festival" of Dai people. In the early morning, all Dai women will get up early to shoulder clean well water or spring water to the Buddhist temple, and clean the dust from the Buddha statue when the sun comes out.

Dai people's ceremony of "bathing the Buddha" is very solemn and grave. They should put in the clean well water or spring water a variety of beautiful and fragrant flowers, pluck green and jady plantain leaves to scoop up the holy pure water, and carefully clean and wipe the Buddha statue until it becomes glittering and spotlessly clean. Apparently people are "washing the Buddha", but in fact they are "washing the mind", devotionally "removing" all kinds of dust and dirt in their own mind and making them pure and bright. With piety, they reproduce the resplendent and magnificent nature of the Buddha statue to pray for blessings and for peace and prosperity of the upcoming year.

Dai girls taking holy water (Jinghong, Yunnan Province)

Chanting sutras is the most important and indispensable ritual activity.

During the Water-Splashing Festival, young people can participate in dancing, splashing water, tossing embroidered parcels, dragon boat racing and other activities, while the elderly of Dai nationality are mainly gathering in the temple to chant sutras or listen to the chanting of the Buddha in the temple. Usually at 7:00 in the morning, they wash themselves at home, and after putting on new clothes, they will go to the temple to worship the Buddha with flowers picked the night before. Some elderly people perfom rap (Rap is the most popular performance among Dai old men; performers need to do it impulsively according to things observed in life, usually in the way of story telling).

The practice of piling up sand is a custom of Dai nationality.

During the festival, people pile with sand three or five gold towers in the courtyard of the Buddhist temple. The towers are more than a meter tall, with several bamboo branches wrapped with strips of red and green cloth inserted in. Then, people sit around the sand towers, and listen to the chanting of monks or the Buddha, praying for good weather and a good harvest in the New Year. Now, "piling

Dai people producing incense
(Mangshi, Yunnan Province)

up sand" has become a folk entertainment or sport activity that can promote mutual understanding, harmony, unity and friendship. Piling up sand is usually held by the river, so as to pray for happiness and joy and avoid disasters and suffering.

The Buddhist culture has a profound influence on Dai nationality. The Dai nationality of Xishuangbanna are all religious believers, who believe in the Southern Sect of Buddhism, also called Hinayana Buddhism. It is said that the the Southern Sect of Buddhism in Xishuangbanna area was introduced by a man named Arzhudalaxi and has a history of more than 1,000 years. Dai people call religion "Shashana"and Buddhism they believe in "Shashana Pazhaogedama".Pazhaogedama refers to the Buddhist leader, Gautama Siddhartha—Sakyamuni. With the development of history, Buddhist culture has gradually been rooted in all aspects of Dai people's life. During such a grand festival like the Water-Splashing Festival, people will invariably express their devotion.

2. The Joyful Water-splashing Ceremony

Water is of great significance to Dai people. Water is a lucky thing, which can wash away the worries, take away diseases and disasters, bring people good luck and happiness in the New Year. Water-splashing is the most lively and most traditional activity during Water-Splashing Festival. It not only implies the auspicious meaning of blessing each other, but also has become more varied and more lively with the development of the time. During the Water-Splashing Festival, the beating of gongs and drums resounds to the sky, and water of blessings splashes everywhere. People dance happily, while yelling out

"Water! Water! Water!"; they splash water onto each other, and bless each other good luck, happiness and health, which is really a spectacular scene.

Every nationality has its own customs, and each custom contains the special meaning of this nationality and expresses gems of wisdom and mental strength. The Water-Splashing Festival is a sacred holiday of Dai people, in which water is regarded as a kind of material with vitality and fertility. This directly reflects Dai people's worship of it, which has become a sacred thing in Dai society. People, without reference to age and sex, irrespective of their high or low birth, all enjoy the joy of the festival. Water splashing is the major traditional activity of the Water-Splashing Festival, and culminates on the second day of the festival. There are many ways of splashing water, mainly divided into traditional water-splashing method and modern water-splashing method. The traditional water-splashing method of Dai nationality is again divided into gentle

Dai girls during the Water-Splashing Festival (Jinghŏng, Yunnan Province)

splashing and wild splashing. The modern water-splashing method mainly centers in some cities or regions where different minorities mix together and celebrate this festival together, which is mainly produced as a result of multicultural interaction.

The Traditional Water-splashing Method

The traditional water-splashing method of Dai nationality is divided into "gentle splashing" and "wild splashing".

The gentle splashing is that Dai people fetch clean water from the well and soak petals and pattra leaves in the water. The petals are mainly those of jasmine, Chinese rose and rose, which make the water smell fragrant when soaked in water. Pattra leaves are what the Buddhists use to copy Buddhist scriptures, and they can ward off evils. Splashing such holy water during the festival is a symbol of good luck and happiness. People carry the water with flower fragrance to the

Dai girls presenting water of blessings (Jinghong, Yunnan Province)

temple, and use the water to clean the dust from the Buddha statue. Then, after dipping the pale green branches into the fragrant water in small basins or small buckets, people lightly sprinkle water on the highly respected or the elders, and then on the young people or those they want to give blessings. The amount of water sprinkled is small, just like the spring drizzle, which usually cannot wet through people's clothes. By gently sprinkling the fresh spring water with light fragrance of flowers, Dai people express their most sincere and beautiful blessings to others and themselves in the New Year.

Dai girls greeting guests at the village during the Water-Splashing Festival
(Ruili, Yunnan Province)

Wild splashing is a popular form among young people, which is usually for peers. The style of wild splashing has no certain standards; people can use big basins or big buckets filled with water to pour towards other poeple's head, face or body, and the splashed can chase and fight back in the same way. According to the traditional culture of Dai nationality, splashing water on each other in the New Year is a symbol of friendship and blessing; those who participate in water splashing are willing to accept others' splashing; and the more they are splashed, the happier they will be. Dai people often say, "During the annual Water-Splashing Festival, splash those whom you have a good opinion of." During the water-splashing activity of the Dai New Year, no matter strangers or acquaintances, Dai people or the foreigners, everyone who comes to participate in the activity will be warmly welcomed and blessed.

The Modern Water-splashing Method

With its increasing influence, the Water-Splashing Festival has covered many cities and villages in Yunnan Province. Now, Han people and other ethnic groups in cities are also involved in the water-splashing flood. For example, in Yunnan Ethnic Village of Kunming, every Dai New Year (April 13 to 15 in

Splashing out the water of happiness (Mengla, Yunnan Province)

solar calendar), there will be a lot of tourists from all over the country to participate in the activities of the Water-Splashing Festival. Carrying large buckets or large pots of water, or shouldering all kinds of water guns, they pour water towards whoever they see. The Water-Splashing Festival draws near the distance between strangers.

Water-Splashing Festival is displayed in cities as a carnival, which someone may feel rough and unacceptable while someone else may feel joyful and worthy of advocating. But in different ways of water splashing, what can be felt is enthusiasm and strong wishes between people. You splash me, and I splash you, water flowers bloom in the air, which symbolize good fortune, happiness and health. The bright and crystal water drops in young people's hands also symbolize sweet love. All the people pour each other, and everywhere is a baptism of water, a blessing of water, and a song of water.

Tips for Tourism

The Water Square in Xishuangbanna

Water—Splashing Festival is the New Year for Dai people in Xish—uangbanna, which is the most solemn Dai festival. There will be such cel—ebrating activities as dragon boat racing, letting off Gaosheng, flying Kong—ming lanterns, water—splashing carnival and *Ganbai*, among which tossing embroidered parcels, national songs and dances and gamecockare impor—tant contents in folk customs. During the Water—Splashing Festival, local people dressed in ethnic costumesand tourists gather in the watersquare in Jinghong City, Xishuangbanna to splash water on each other. The water square is the central landmark building of Jinghong and also the main venue for the annual Water—Splashing Festival. Located in the south of Jinghong, beside the transit road and near the Lancang River and Daijiangnan night market. The fountain in the middle of the square and the statue in the front embody the elements of Water—Splashing Festival. Every April and May, if visiting the site in person, you can feel the enthusiasm and delight of splashing and being splashed. At the same time, in big streets or small al—leys of Jinghong City, every Dai village, especially Ganlanba, there will be water—splashing activities.

Matters needing attention

During the Water—Splashing Festival, temperature varies greatly from morning to evening in Jinghong City, so it is necessary for those who will participate in the water—splashing activities to bring two outfits for change in case of being soaked through. Better not to carry a mobile phone or camera with you unless it is waterproof enough; try not to make noises, not to fight for water; do not use dirty water or sewage, and splash water in a civilized way.

Best travel time

"Hot" is a feature of the climate of Xishuangbanna. The annual av—erage temperature here is 21.9℃ and there are dry season and rainy season. November to May is the dry season, with cool weather, and is the peak season for tourism. Especially in April, there is the grand Water—Splashing Festival. June to October is the rainy season, the weather being hot and humid, but it is a good time to taste all kinds of fruits. And because there are fewer visitors, the travelling expenses may also decline.

3. The Unique National Competitive Entertainment

During the Water-Splashing Festival, in addition to expressing blessings with splashing water, people will also hold such activities as letting off Gaosheng, flying Kongming lanterns, dragon boat racing, beauty contest, bamboo raft rac-ing, crossbow shooting competition, the game of whipping tops, selecting King of fruitsand the game of eating watermelons. Through competition, the cohesive force of a nation is displayed, and the purest disposition and supplication of the people are released incisively and vividly.

Letting off Gaosheng

Gaosheng is a homemade firework of Dai people. In the minds of the local people, the higher the Gaosheng of a village flies, the more glorious and auspicious the village will be. So the person whose Gaosheng flies the highest will be appreciated by the people. The competition of letting off Gaosheng is a battle of wisdom.

On the first day of the New Year, one of the most important activities is to let off Gaosheng, heralding the coming of a new day. Gaosheng, called "Mangfei" in Dai language, is a kind of primitive rocket that appeared at an earlier time, which is made from gunpowder packed in a bamboo tube. On the eve of the festival, people usually put up with bamboo poles a shelf of several zhang (a unit of length, one-third metres high) as the launch pad in the open space or square. On the day of the Water-Splashing Festival, Gaosheng is put on the top of the bamboo shelf; after being let off, "Mangfei" will fly up to the sky holding white smoke and dragging a long tail. With the rise of "Mangfei", people in the festival costumes will knock on the gongs, beat the elephant-foot drum, and jump joyously. They will also perform Peacock Dance and sing the local folk songs. With the soaring sound of Gaosheng, the scene is full of the crowds' excitement. The maker of "Mangfei" that flies the highest will be admired and praised by people, and will also get some material rewards.

Dai people are very skilled in making Gaosheng. They fill a handful of bamboo tubes with charcoal, sulfur, and nitre, and make them into powder barrels. The power barrels are then bound to a slender bamboo pole and placed on a pre-built bamboo launch pad, and will fly up to the sky with white smoke after the fuse lit. Gaosheng is divided into different types as a single set, double sets and multiple sets: only one powder barrel bound to a long bamboo pole is called a single set, two powder barrels bound to a long bamboo pole are called double sets, and multiple powder barrels bound to the bamboo poleare called multiple sets. A single set, double sets and multiple sets are distinguished by the number of powder barrels, while the long bamboo pole, which is a part of Gaosheng, has only one. When the first powder barrel burns out, the second powder barrel will start burning, and continue to push Gaosheng to the upper air. And so will the third powder barrel. As a result, Gaosheng will fly higher.

Flying Kongming Lanterns

The Kongming lantern, also called "flying light", and "Gongfei" in Dai language, is a kind of flying "paper balloon" created by Dai people in Xishuangbanna. It is said to have been invented after Buddhism was introduced to Xishuangbanna. At the time, Buddhists competed with folk religious believers to see whose making fly the highest. Folk religious believers made Gaosheng flying up to the sky, while Buddhist disciples produced a fire fly light. As the flaming paper lanterns fly into the tranquil night sky, the crowds looking up on the ground are cheering, singing and dancing to celebrate the New Year. The Kongming lantern is a symbol of good luck, happiness and pride for Dai people.

Dragon-boat Racing

Dragon-boat racing is usually held on "Maipayawanma"

(the third day) of the Water-Splashing Festival. People wearing festival costumes gather around the Lancang River, Ruili River and Yingjiang River to watch the dragon-boat race. The dragon boat is painted exquisite color lines; and there is a bamboo pole with a colored ribbon on the tail of the carved wooden dragon. Several valiant rowers sit on it. In the race, the person standing in the middle of the boat is in charge by knocking the gong, and in the specified range, the team that gets to the destination first will win the race. With the gong knocked, the dragon boats ready for the challenge fly forward like arrows. And then the whole river resounds with the corresponding sounds of drums, gongs, work songs and cheers, which push the festive atmosphere to a climax. The dragon boat race is usually carried out with one village fighting against another. The winning team will receive the banner and the prize, as well as congratulations and cheers of people. By taking advantage of the festive scene at the end of the dragon boat race, people will play gongs and elephant-foot drums, and perform the traditional Dai dance for celebration.

Beauty Contest

The beauty contest is one of the most fascinating events in the Water-Splashing Festival. The girl who can win the final game must be generally recognized as both beautiful and intelligent. Participants in the race are usually qualified to enter the final election after preselection. After the competitive sport of stage show and talent show, the girl who wins the most applause of the audience and the most favor of the judges will be the final "water girl", meaning the girl is as beautiful as water. The beauty contest in the Water-Splashing Festival has added vividness and colorfulness to the Water-Splashing

Festival.

Cross-bow Shooting

Cross-bow is one of the oldest weapons in the world. It is a tool for hunting, fighting and self-defense to the ancient ethnic groups in such Chinese regions as Yunnan, Guizhou and Sichuan Province. Cross-bow shooting competition of Dai nationality is divided into two groups: standing position and kneeling position, both of which are unsupported. As an ethnic sports item present in the Water-Splashing Festival, it adds to the festival a festival atmosphere.

Cross-bow shooting by the Lisu nationality at the festival

The Game of Whipping Tops

Whipping tops is a popular sports activity among Dai people. Under the lead of the local culture sector, people should apply first and then compete. In the game, the competitor holds a bamboo stick with thread in right hand and the lower part of the top in left hand, then wrap the thread around the top and the left hand casts off the top, while the right hand gently pulls it to make it rotate on the ground. The opponent uses the same method, and should hit the spinning top. When the two rotating tops collide, the one that is still spinning will win the game.

Selecting King of Fruits

Due to the advantages of geographical condition, the living area of Dai nationality is rich in watermelons, bananas and so on. During the Water-Splashing Festival, every village will take the largest watermelon and heaviest banana for competition. "King of Watermelon"and "King of Banana" will be selected, and the winners will be encouraged by a bonus. "All kinds of Kings" will be invited to different villages to teach the planting experience next year.

The Game of Eating Watermelons

The game of eating watermelons is the most exciting and stressful event during the Water-Splashing Festival. In order to make the guests feel the charm of Dai villages, sometimes the organizing committee of Water-Splashing Festival will hold the game of eating watermelons. The watermelon feast is made up of watermelons that run for "King of Watermelon" in the morning. There is no difference of men or women in the watermelon match, and no limit to the number of attending people either. Whoever finishes eating the prescribed amount in the prescribed time will be the winner. The gobbling up of "King of Eating Watermelons" attracts cheers and laughter from the spectators now and then, adding an unlimited amount of fun to the festival.

4. The Interesting Custom of "Tossing embroidered parcels"

The Water-Splashing Festival is also a great time for many single men and women to seek love and find life partners. At the time of the festival, young men and women feel unusually happy. Their anticipation of "Tossing embroidered parcels" can be seen from their being busy making embroidered parcels and choosing beautiful clothes long before the festival. One or two weeks before the Water-Splashing Festival, Dai girls will start to sew beautiful embroidered parcels, for which they usually choose bright-colored cloth. For lots of single young people, "Tossing embroidered parcels" may be a very easy thing, which is the process of throwing and picking up. But making beautiful embroidered parcels in person will be a difficult task. So before the Water-Splashing Festival, some Dai girls will take along the beautiful cloth and needlework carefully chosen by them, and gather together to learn the craftsmanship from those senior people or elders who can make embroidered parcels. Because it is an important love-harvesting activity, they lay stress on each stitch. The sewing stitches reflect the patience and carefulness of Dai girls' character, and the embroidered parcels finally made are very beautiful too.

Dai girls and boys choose beautiful clothes on the festival day, prepare some gifts, get dressed up, and meet together to play the game of "Tossing embroidered parcels" at an open space. It is usually divided into two groups, girls on the one side, boys on the other side, with a boy and a girl throwing at each other. The side that cannot catch the parcel will be punished by the other side. The methods of the punishment vary, of course, and a lot of them are what they plot well in advance, while some are out of temporary thoughts. Usually if a boy fails to get the girl's parcel, he will give the prepared gift to the girl, or put the prepared flowers on the head of the girl. On the contrary, if a girl fails to catch a boy's parcel, she would have to put the flowers on the boy's chest to be a present for the boy. This is how a romantic love story begins with a moving embroidered parcelas a way of communication.

5. The Passionate Dances

Singing and dancing mix together; singing can be melodious, expressing feelings and meanings, but dancing is not to be outdone. Dai people are good at singing and dancing, and have a lot of talents, so the Water-Splashing Festival cannot go well without them. Beautiful costumes, joyous crowds, smooth and free body movements, all bear the most natural language expression. People learn from peacocks' elegance and refinement, and emulate elephants' steadiness and steadfast. Accompanied by music, the dancing is sometimes slow and romantic, sometimes bright and light, and with every smile and every move, emotion flows like water, naturally.

Peacock Dance

Peacock Dance is called "Ga Luoyong" in Dai language. "Luoyong" means peacock, and "Ga" means dance. Peacock Dance is one of the most beautiful and most popular dances of Dai people. The rich and beautiful land where Dai people live has always enjoyed the reputation of "The Land of Peacocks". In the past, at the time of morning twilight or sun setting, peacocks with beautiful posture can often be seen dancing trippingly. Therefore, peacock is a symbol of good fortune, happiness, beauty and kindness in Dai people's heart. At the time of a festival, Dai people will gather together to watch Peacock Dance performed by folk artists and adapted from folk stories, myths, legends and Buddhist stories, or dance about peacocks' behavior. For example, the Peacock Dance based on the fairy tale "The devil and the peacock" is still very popular now among the people. It tells of the story that the devil would commandeer the peacock as wife, while the peacock with a human face and bird's body struggled to shake her beautiful feathers, whose bright radiance made the devil brothers blind, and the peacock won.

The Peacock Dance originated from a beautiful legend.

It is said that in the ancient times, there lived in the forest a group of happy and lovely peacock spirits that were good at singing and dancing. As soon as they danced, the whole forest was jubilant. One day, two demons came from nowhere, declaring that the forest was their territory and demanded the beautiful peacock princess to be their "queen". The peacock princess pretended to be happy and asked the devils to marry her in the palace of the peacock kingdom. She walked and flew, leading the devil to the swampland on the edge of the forest. The devils were swallowed up by the mud and the forest was restored to peace. The peacock princess sang and danced, and the forest was full of joy again. This is only a beautiful myth circulating among Dai people, who compared Dai village to the forest, while the peacock princess was the embodiment of kindness and courage, who eliminated the evil with wisdom and saved the whole forest.

Peacock Dance is a kind of property dance performed in the square during grand festivals or "Zuobai" (the Buddhist meeting for the cultivation of merit and virtue), generally performed by 1 or 2 or 3 people. But as a result of Dai nationality being divided into different branches, the spread and development of Peacock Dance in different regions are also different. Therefore, although Peacock Dance has a unified performance formula, it is not in one pattern. Peacock Dance in different Dai regions is very much the same, although each has its own expertise. The Peacock Dance in Xishuangbanna still keeps the dance of two people symbolizing a male and female peacock, and wearing a mask and a peacock frame, and the performance is fairly traditional. Peacock Dance in Ruili area is characterised as imitating peacocks' various expressions and actions, such as "flying down the mountain", "peeping in the forest", "wandering in the forest", "drinking and playing with spring water", "chasing and playing", "spreading wings", "trailing wings", "stiring wings", "dapping" and other elegant dancing posture. Its props are light, the skill is demanding, and there are many folk artists performing it. In the area of Mangshi, Peacock Dance is mainly galloping in quick short steps, turning in the place, and the introflexion of the arms and palming. The dancers' use of quick short steps and hand movements is rare in other areas. The above mentioned are the forms and characteristics of Dai Peacock Dance of different areas. The differences between them are not big, only some special characteristics in some small details.

The Peacock Dance has a rich style and outstanding characteristics, expressing implicit sentiment, and the posture has a sense of sculpture. The dance is mainly performed through the joints of the body parts like the head, hands, fingers, arms, upper arms, lower arms, elbow, shoulder, waist, hip, knees and so on, with the bones being as curving as possible. Various body movements, graceful S shape, the teasing, pushing, pulling, withdrawing, and swaying of hands or the jump, moving, appel, running, tiptoeing of feet shifting with the movement rhythm, or the stretch and flow of beautiful modelling in Peacock Dance, all represent the distinctive personality of peacocks. Peacock Dance can make people feel not only the natural rhythm of beautiful landscape, but also the peace, simplicity and originality of Dai people. It also makes people feel Dai people's understanding of beauty and desire for sweet life.

The most representative and expressive Dai dance is Spirit of Peacock by Yang Liping, which lasts nearly 7 minutes. From the start to the end of the dance, the shape and stateof her upper body is basically "three curves", namely, the force is out of the front and back of the waist and chest, and through the three curves of the upper body and the exaggerating swinging range of the hip, the most original, authentic, natural and simple basic modelling of a beautiful peacock standing on the top branch and ready to fly is presented. As a unique form in Dai dances, "three curves" mainly presents Dai women's gracefulness like water, gentility, slenderness and elegance.

Yi Shun Bian(Leaning on the same side)

The dancing posture of "Yi Shun Bian" is extracted from the basic dancing movement rhythm of stretching and placidity inherent in Dai dances, mainly presenting the dancing intention of peace and comfort, desire and happiness. Although most Dai people reside in dykes, the geographic area and geographical location of plateau mountain directly afffect the working people's gait and dynamic movement in daily work and family life labor as well. The mountain roads are rough, and people have many inconveniences going back and forth.

Needless to say going uphill and downhill, even the general walk is greatly different from that in the plains, which mainly lies in the acting point of the sole and the balance of the body, and gradually the posture of "Yi Shun Bian"is formed.

The Elephant-foot Drum

The elephant-foot drum is one of the most important dance instruments of the Water-Splashing Festival. The elephant-foot drums of Dai people have three sizes: long, medium and small. There are not many movements in the long elephant-foot drum dance, which is good at beating variation and rich drumbeat. There are beating with one finger, two fingers, three fingers, a palm, a fist, an elbow, foot, the head and so on. It is performed usually by one person or accompanying the dance. The long elephant-foot drum is the highest of elephant-foot drums, called "Guangya" in Dai language, usually 130cm to 160cm high, with the highest 190cm and the drum head 30cm in diameter. The medium elephant-foot drum is usually beaten with a fist, or with a mallet in some regions. There is no more drumbeat, usually one pat, one beat, with the left finger adding weak beat in some areas. The length of drumbeat, the pitch of the tone and the swinging size of the drum tail are regarded as the standard. It is said that the lasting sound of one beat is enough to unbutton the clothes, and to buckle all buttons with another beat before the drum sound finishes. The medium elephant-foot drum dance is steady and strong, with more large movements and large postures. The number of dancers is not limited, beating in pair with few people and beating in a circle with more people. The medium drum, called "Guangtun" in Dai language, is the most widely used in the elephant-foot drums and often used in the elephant-foot drum dance or festive celebrations. The drum is 60cm to 95cm high, the drum head 23cm to 28cm in diameter, the drum bottom 23cm to 31cm in diameter, and the thinnest part of the waist 11cm to 15cm in diameter. The small elephant-foot drum is only often seen in Xishuangbanna, the dancing movements being flexible and leaping, and is characterized as drum game and drum contest. In the game and the contest, the one that can flexibly and wittingly attack, retreat, and finally grasp the other's hat or turban will win. Usually it is held in pairs. The small drum looks like a short cup, only 30cm to 40 cm high, and is not used as widely as large, and medium-sized drums.

The Elephant-foot Drum Dance

The elephant-foot drum dance plays an important role in the Water-Splashing Festival. Men in Xishuangbanna, from the juvenile, the youth to the elder people, can all perform the elephant-foot drum dance. In general, a man is leading the dance while beating a drum, while others successively join the dance team, lifting foot and dancing according to the powerful drumbeat. Some elephant-foot drum dance also needs singing while dancing. The dance team gradually expands, and at the time of its climax, the scene is lively, powerful and magnificent. Men performing the elephant-foot drum dance wear long drums covered with cowhide at both sides and shaped like an elephant foot. There is a ribbon or figured cloth on the waist of the drum, which is slung over the dancer's shoulder, and the dancer is drumming while dancing. With the warm and happy rhythm, the dancers' feet step the ground strongly, both knees bend and straighten alternatively, and their bodies rise and fall, like elephants strolling in the jungle. Their steps are steady and strong, and their dance easy and free.

Tips for Tourism

The Singing and Dancing Performances of Dai People in Xishuangbanna

If travelling in Xishuangbanna for the first time, you can experience the wonderful singing and dancing performances there. During the Water-Splashing Festival, both the peacock dance and the elephant-foot drum dance will be performed. During the ordinary days of Xishuangbanna, you can also enjoy the enthusiastic folk dance in Manting Park, Dai Garden of Xishuangbanna or Mengbalanaxi Art Palace, among which the large-scale singing and dancing performances of *The Night of Langcang-Mekong River Mengbalanaxi* are prominent.

6. The Unique Dai Costumes

On the day of the Water-Splashing Festival, all the Dai people will put on beautiful festival costumes, singing and dancing, and splash water on each other for blessings. Dai boys are simple and generous, with a scarf on head and straps on back, and a small short-sleeved shirt matching a wide-waist and no-pocket pants of pure color. Dai girls are in light yellow, wearing tight jackets and gorgeous barrel skirts, with graceful, free and light behavior.

The Costumes of Dai Women

The habitation of Dai people is the barrage area of a sub-tropical rainforest climate, where the weather is hot, the rainfall is abundant, the plants are flourishing, the lakes are interlaced and the rivers are criss-crossed. Dai people living here are slender, small and delicate. Dai girls like wearing short jackets with narrow cuffs and flowery tight skirts. This kind of skirt is ankle-length and waist-height, tightly wrapping the lower part of the body, which fully shows the streamline beauty of women's BWH (bust, waist, hips). Besides, the drapery adopted is soft, bright and lively, which can not only highlight the charm of women, but also give their slender figure a full display, graceful, elegant, natural and unrestrained. Women's costumes vary greatly from place to place, but the barrel skirt is popular almost among all Dai nationality. The skirt, also called "tube skirt", has got its name for having no folds and looking like a round tube. The barrel skirt will naturally remind people of Dai girls' pretty image of wearing skirts, and for this reason, it has become one of the symbols of Dai nationality.

There are differences in the costumes of Dai women in different areas.

The traditional costumes of Dai women in Xishuangbanna are the black long-sleeve right-lapel and round-collar tight jacket, the front edge decorated with several color strips, and the black tight skirt from the waist to the instep, wrapped tightly by a silver belt, the upper part of the skirt woven predominantly with dark red color strips. The costumes of modern women are colorful and various in style, such as condole belt type and circular collar type. The hair style, regardless of the young or the old, is a bun in the back of the head or a loosely deviated bun at the upper rightpart of the back of head, with decorations like small and exquisite hair combs or hairpins. The costumes of Dai people in Xishuangbanna are more innovative and colorful.

The traditional costumes of Dai women in Jinping are a white double-breasted waist-high long-sleeved tight garment, older women also in blue or light blue, and a black barrel skirtto the instep, with the hem laced with color lacework.They fasten a green or scarlet silk belt around the waist; the buttons are silver and double-breasted with butterfly patterns, which is the distinctive feature of the costumes of this ethnic group. Long coats are black, similar to wind coats, mostly worn by older women. Modern costumes have no big changes, basically keeping the traditional style and colours. From the whole, the costumes' style of Dai people in Jinping tends to be traditional, and the colours are elegant, predominantly black and white, other colours as decorations.

The graceful Dai girls (Mengla, Yunnan Province)

The Costumes of Dai Men

Compared with Dai women still wearing the traditional costumes of Dai nationality in daily life, labor and festivals, the costumes of Dai men have changed greatly. No matter in Jinping or Dehong and Xishuangbanna, the costumes of Dai men basically have no big differences from those of Han nationality; they wear traditional costumes only in some important festivals such as Water-Splashing Festival or important occasions. But in the past, the costumes of Dai men reflected the ecological environment of living beside the water. Men will wrap their heads in white or light blue cloth, usually wear white or black shirts and straight pants with wider trouser legs. The colors of the shirt and pants are often the same, and the borders of the garments will also be embroidered some patterns and laces in gold thread. The color of Dai men's costumes is generally simple and elegant, slightly dim. That Men's trouser legs are wide is related to the fact that they often touch water and river. When crossing the river, they can easily roll up the pants, and to a very high place, and the pants can quickly become dry after being splashed wet by holy water of blessings during the Water-Splashing Festival.

Tattooing

In the ancient texts, no accounts about the ancients of Dai nationality will not mention their custom of tattooing. Tattoos are the most characteristic body decorations of Dai people, and also one of the important symbols of becoming Dai nationality. Long time ago, this custom of decorating the body should be followed by all Dai men, otherwise they would be rejected by the society. It is recorded in *A Record of Baiyi* (Dai nationality was called Baiyi in ancient times), "The hair of Baiyi should be shaved, and shins be tattooed; those whose hair is not shaved will be killed, while those with no tattoos will be mocked and compared to women."

Tattoos are more commonly seen in men, and there are few women with tattoos. Even if some women do have, they usually tattoo in the wrist or arm some simple patterns, or their own names, or some Buddhist scriptures. There is no strict age limit for tattooing, but usually between 12 and 30. There are no strict limits on the parts of the body tattooed either; every part of the body is fine. The ancient tattooing of Dai nationality has different classes, which can be used to distinguish social status. It is recorded in *An Introduction to Southwest Minorities* that "Men are demanded by law to be tattooed at the lower part of the body. To distinguish their social status, Buyi (ordinary people) can be tattooed to the leg, Muba (inferior leaders) can be tattooed to the waist, and Tuguan (the chief leader) can be tattooed to the breast." The noble men can choose red patterns, while ordinary people can only choose black or pelious designs. The tattooed patterns include the shape of animals, mainly that of tigers, lions, elephants, dragons, peacocks, birds, snakes and so on; and words, simple Buddhist scriptures, names of people and Buddhas; and also lines, patterns, water ripples, lines, circles, and so on.

There are generally two ways of tattooing. One is to use a sharp object like a needle or a blade to prick the skin or carve a variety of desired patterns, then paint them. The other is to twine a needle tip with some thread or gauze,the needle tip exposed, and directly prick into the skin by dipping in the paint and ink. When the paint in the gauze becomes dry, dip again until a complete pattern is finished.

According to Dai people, tattoos are not only important adornments and a sign of decency, but more importantly, in their religious idea, tattoos can protect them against ghosts, harm and evil. Men become more courageous and responsible after being tattooed, and turn into attractive men.

Teeth Decorating

Teeth decorating includes teeth dyeing and teeth inserting, both of which rely on other substances to change the color of teeth. Teeth dyeing of Dai people in Xishuangbanna and Jinping is very much the same, which generally includes two kinds of methods: one is to fumigate the chestnut wood until it smokes, then smoke a small piece of iron and dye teeth by using tobacco-juice on the iron by hand; the other is through the long-term chewing of plants, which turns the teeth from red to black, and the color will not fade away. The latter method is different in the two places: Dai people in Jinping chew a kind of ivy leaf plant locally called "Bu", mixed with straw smoke or lime, while Dai people in Xishuangbanna area mainly chew betel nuts. Teeth inserting is to make tooth sockets with metal pieces and then inlay them on the front teeth, which become "gold teeth" or "silver teeth". Both men and women follow the custom of teeth inserting, while teeth dyeing is mainly done among married women.

7. The Delicious Dai Food

The food culture of Dai people has experienced a long history, and enjoys an important position in Chinese cuisine promenade. Its distinct characteristics of both adapting to the ecological environment and having the spirit of humanism have gained it great popularity in Chinese food industry. Dai flavor is not only popular in Dai areas; there are also many people who like it in some cities. Before the Water-Splashing Festival, Dai people will be busy killing pigs and chickens, making wine, and preparing barbecue ingredients. They will also make a lot of "hao nuo suo' (rice cake) and a variety of Baba made of glutinous rice, and gather all kinds of fresh fruits and edible wild herbs for the festival. The traditional food culture of Dai people has distinct characteristics.

Highlighting the Sour and the Spicy Flavour

Dai people love sour and spicy flavor, which has a lot to do with the hot climate and humid air of their residence. The heat of the climate tends to affect people's appetites, while sour is not only refreshing, appetizing, digestive, but also getting rid of the fishy odor. Sour food is not easy to grow bad in hot areas, so sour bamboo shoots cooked together with chicken, fish and cured beef, and lemon chicken salad are all Dai delicacies popular for their sour flavor. Eating spicy food has dehumidifying power, and can reduce the pain of rheumatism. Dai people especially like to cook dishes with fresh Xiaomi pepper (small but very spicy pepper), and Dai-flavor barbecue, baoshao, dipping sauce cannot do without spicy flavor. We can say, no spicy flavor, no Dai flavor; there is even the saying that "It's not a Dai dish without spicy flavor".

Enjoying Glutinous Rice Food

Dai nationality is one of the earliest nationalities in China to grow rice. Dai people in different areas mainly eat rice, and glutinous rice is the staple food of Dai people. Hot and cold glutinous rice are both delicious, and in order to seize time, Dai people often bring glutinous rice as lunch when going to work in the fields. During the growing season, Dai women will get up early to steam the glutinous rice soaked the night before, and then put them into a bamboo basket after encasing them with plantain leaves (some are put in the lunch box made of plaited bamboo strips), and bring some pickled vegetables, sauce, fried beef jerky before going out to work. At noon, they have lunch while sitting at the field edge. Glutinous rice is elastic, which is not only soft and delicious, but also chewy, resistance to hunger, non-greasy and difficult to fall down, so it is greatly favored by Dai people. They believe that eating glutinous rice can make girls slim and young men good at jumping and running.

Glutinous rice is not only a staple food for Dai people, but also an important supplementary ingredient in making a series of complementary food. For example, "hao nuo suo", "hao beng", "hao men", "hao bang", and "hao bang lu" are the most common glutinous rice products. At the time of the Dai New Year, every Dai household will make a lot of these kinds of food, for self-eating or selling to others or sending to friends or relatives. "Hao nuo suo" is equivalent to the rice cake of Han nationality. Dai people say, "Men are one year older after eating Hao nuo suo". There is also pineapple sticky rice, fragrant and sweet, which is regarded as a special skill of Dai food. Bamboo-tube-cooked rice is also a cate favored by Dai people, cooked by putting the soaked glutinous rice in bamboo tubes and then steaming or boiling them. It not only keeps the original fragrance of glutinous rice, but also adds the faint scent of bamboos.

The Rich Pickles and Sauces

Dai people who love eating pickles and are good at making pickles. There are many kinds of pickles, not only pickled vegetables such as pickled radish and pickled cabbage, but also salted pork, salted beef and salted fish. These pickles are both sour and spicy, especially in the taste of Dai people, who may prepare a small bowl of pickles to go with rice, or cook together with other vegetables with the pickles as ingredients.

The sour and spicy flavor is both appetizing and helping eat more. Sauce is called "Nanmi" in Dai language. At the dinner table of Dai people, there can be no meat, but there cannot be without Nanmi. Nanmi has rich varieties, and different vegetables dip different Nanmi, including "Nanmi bu" (crab sauce), "Nanmi pa" (vegetable sauce), "Nanmi maheisong" (tomato sauce), "Nanmi ruo" (bamboo shoots sauce), "Nanmi mapi"(hot pepper sauce), "Nanmi ba" (fish sauce), "Nanmi tuoling"(peanut butter), "Nanmi mage"(Galiluo sauce) and so on. As Dai Zanha (Dai folk singer) sings, "Eating without Nanmi is just like living without love, and the days are plain and dull". It can be seen that Nanmi plays an important role in the food culture of Dai people.

Preference to Wild Vegetables and Vegetarian Dishes

Dai nationality is a nation that dares to explore and try what is edible and what is not edible among wild vegetables. They will always find various kinds of wild vegetables in the traditional way, and after many people's foretaste, leave valuable experience for their offspring. Through the experience of the grandparents and the constant exploration of the younger generation, Dai people have learnt many edible wild vegetables, and more than 90 kinds of them can be called by name.

Green moss, a natural "green algae" in Dai food, is taken from the river and then sun-dried after frying them into thin pancakes. It can be fried with oil, or with chopped green onion or cooking oil and salt after being crushed. When eating glutinous rice, grasp a pinch of green moss and nip in the rice; the fresh green color and the fragrant and exquisite flavor will increase people's appetite.

Mixed vegetable is another favorite home cooking of Dai

people. It is a soup by cooking several kinds of vegetables together, which is said to be quite nutritious for the variety of vegetables involved. Several vegetables are usually cooked together: amaranth, pumpkin tip, little cabbage, beet leaves, and a dash of eruka siata, Xiaomi pepper and shredded ginger. Put some salt but no oil during cooking; the color of the soup is green and clear, and the aroma of various plants is mixed together, which produces a distinctive taste.

Dai people like to plant lentils and winged beans next to the walls of their courtyard. Pick the fresh bean pods and boil in clean water, scoop out in a bowl, mix with peanut butter and a natural flavor is ready. In addition, water cilantro, cabbage, fennel, mint, acanthopanax, wild eggplant, cucumber, Houttuynia cordata are the vegetables that Dai people eat raw by dipping in the sauce. Grilled eggplants and leek eaten together with dipping sauce have a unique taste. Dai people like vegetarian food, partly because their cooking methods greatly preserve the aroma and vitamins of the plants, and partly because the sauce is sour and spicy, which makes the refreshing and strong vegetarian diet the most appropriate in the hot and humid regions of Dai nationality. Therefore, in addition to festivals, Dai people usually have vegetarian diet in their daily life. Compared with Han nationality, Dai people eat vegetables in a different way. Han people's cooking methods for vegetables are mainly boiling or frying, while Dai people prefer eating raw or dipping sauces after boiling in hot water. Compared with stir-fry in much oil, Dai people's cooking is more tasty and refreshing.

Diverse Cooking Methods

One important feature of Dai diet culture is the variety of cooking methods, which include barbecuing, Baoshao (barbecuing after wrapping up), steaming, chopping, salting, pounding, deep frying, frying, boiling, salad making and so on.

"Barbecuing" is one of the most common culinary arts in Dai cuisine culture. Dai people prefer the way of barbecuing when having meat, and these dishes include barbecued fish with lemongrass, barbecued chicken with lemongrass, barbecued pork, barbecuedcured beef and so on. Before barbecuing, carefully choose the materials, add a lot of ingredients and seasoning, and the fire also needs to be mastered well. In this way, the barbecued meat can look golden but not burnt, taste crisp outside while tender inside.

Baoshao is also a common cooking method of Dai food. Dai people first season the vegetables with a variety of sauces, then wrap the seasoned vegetables with banana leaves, hold with two iron racks, and stir and roast on hot coals. When the leaves are burnt into black, the vegetables inside are done. The dishes cooked in this way taste tender and delicious. On the one hand, the leaves lock the original moisture of the vegetables and keep them fresh. On the other hand, Baoshao is grilling on the coals separated by plantain leaves, so the aroma of barbecues and plantain leaves is added. The main dishes of Baoshao are Baoshao pork, Baoshao beef, Baoshao fish, and Baoshao vegetables and so on. Different from Baoshao, among Dai people of Dehong, there is also a special dish eaten by every household during festivals: roasting-meat rice noodles. When cooking it, cut the streaky pork at the pig's belly into large thin slices, and souse with salt, wine, MSG, pepper, soy sauce, spices, and then grill on the big fire after skewering the meat. After cooking the meat well, take it down and cut up, then put in peameal and rice noodles, add such ingredients as salt, MSG, coriander, mashed garlic, soy sauce, chili oil, sesame oil, and peanut sauc. And the most important step is to put in "sour water" specially made by Dai people, then stir well and it can be served.

Barbecued Chicken with Lemongrass of Dai ethnic gnup

Deepfried dishes are mainly deepfried bamboo worms, deepfried fish, deepfried pork skin, deepfried green moss and deepfried rice cakes. Fried dishes are mainly fried eggs with green moss, fried eggs with green peppers, and fried beef slices. The difference between deepfrying and frying is that the former is done in a pot of much oil, while the latter usually does not require much oil. The oil used in both methods is usually colza oil, because dishes cooked in it looks better.

Dai people have both wooden steamers and iron steamers. Wooden steamers are used for steaming rice while iron steamers for steaming vegetables. Because the steamed rice and dishes are fresh, tender and delicious, and not easy to produce excessive internal heat, they are suitable to all people without reference to age and sex. Dai people steam pineapples of tropical fruits and rice together, and "pineapple rice" made in this way is quite popular. The taste of pineapples is sweet, which is suitable for promoting appetite. The pineapple rice is rich in nutrition, and the cooking method is simple, so it has become a favored staple food of Dai peple and tourists of other ethnic groups as well. Besides steamed rice, dishes cooked by steaming are mainly steamed ham, steamed sausage, steamed cured beef, steamed fish, steamed eggs and so on. Dai people mainly steam some meat diet that can easily produce excessive internal heat after being sun-dried.

The dishes cooked in the way of "boiling" are boiled green vegetables, sour bamboo shoots and chicken, sour bamboo shoots and fish, field snail, Niupahu (hot and well-cooked beef soup) and so on. Dai people like sour flavor, and whenever boiling dishes, they will put in sour bamboo shoots, tomatoes or sour fruits (pickled papaya, sour eggplants). For example, when boiling vegetables, especially bitter vegetables, called "Suanpacai" in Dai language, wash vegetables clean and do not cut, wring them by hand into 4 to 5 cm long, put into the boiling water, at the same time add a little shredded ginger and a tomato (or sour bamboo shoots and other sour fruits), do not put in oil and salt. After the dish is cooked, eat together with sauce dip; its taste is light but appetizing.

Duosheng is usually made from fresh beef or pork, being pounded or finely chopped up. There are three kinds: one is eaten with seasoning, another is chopping into thin slices but not boiled, the third is eaten after chopping into thin slices and boiling. The dishes cooked in the way of "chopping" are pork Duosheng, beef Duosheng, fish Duosheng, muntjac meat

Duosheng and so on. According to Dai people, all meat can be cooked into Duosheng. "Duosheng" is a famous dish that goes with wine, which is sweet, sour and spicy.

The salting method is divided into two types: cooked salting and uncooked salting. There are dozens of dishes cooked in the salting method such as salted beef tendons, salted cattle hide, salted pettitoes, salted fish, salted shredded bamboo shoots, salted vegetables, salted ferns and so on. The commonly seen "sour water" in Dai and other ethnic groups, the traditional sauce dip used in the meal, is made in the method of "salting". Here is the method: in the twelfth month of the lunar year, uproot the turnips and dry them, infuse them in the boiled glutinous rice porridge mixed with water, stir every day until it turns sour. The sour water is then scooped out into a pot, and boiled until it thickens to become "sour water". Pickled turnips can still be put in the sour water in the pot, boiled and dried, which become "dried pickles" and can be used as sour soup. Continue to boil the "sour water" left until it thickens and becomes a paste, namely, "pickle paste". When there is no "sour water", take it out and concoct with water, and mix with cold dishes. This kind of "sour water" can be eaten all year round.

Dishes cooked in the way of "pounding" include a variety of Nanmi sauces. For example, the crab sauce is made by pounding the crab meat into minces, boiling it in the pot until it thickens and becomes a paste, and then removing it out and drying in the sun. Before eating, chop up the ingredients such as green pepper, garlic, green onions and put in a bowl, and add a piece of dry crab paste and right amount of boiling water and salt, then after grinding it into powder with pounding salt rod, it can be served for dipping glutinous rice, which tastes spicy and delicious. In addition, it is the home cooking of Dai people to peel the grilled eggplants and tomatoes, then mix with some ingredients like green onions, ginger, garlic, coriander, pepper, salt and pound into powder. Modern families mostly use electric appliances, which is not convenient for grilling, so people usually steam or boil eggplants and tomatoes first, peel them, pound into powder after adding various ingredients, which also tastes good.

The cold dishes mainly include lemon chicken, lemon sa, bitter sa, cucumber salad, pigskin salad, and cold Houttuynia and so on. "Lemon chicken" is one of the most popular dishes in Dai flavor; the scent and sour of lemons matching the spicy flavor of Xiaomi pepper make lemon chicken the most appetizing and refreshing meat dish. "niu sa pie" is also one of the most distinctive dishes of Dai nationality. It has two kinds: "sour sa" and "bitter sa", whose difference lies in that one is sour and hot, while the other is bitter and hot. The "bitter sa" does not use lemons, but the bitter water in cattle's stomach. After slaughtering the cattle, filter the inside of the stomach with gauze until the liquid flows out, then boil the liquid in the pot (the purpose is for sterilization), and it can be used to mix "bitter sa" after turning cold.

Home-brewed Rice Wine

Wine is not only a drink that can eliminate humidity, keep out the cold and reduce fatigue, but also a delicacy for entertaining guests for Dai people. In the heart of Dai people, it is not a feast without wine; even if when eating pickles, they would feel happy with wine. They love to drink home-brewed rice wine; they will put the brewed rice wine in terrines, place in a cool place, wait for the festive season to invite relatives and friends mutually to taste wonderful food and wine. They greet guests with wine, dance with wine, and deepen friendship with wine.

Fresh Fruits

The residential areas of Dai people are mostly tropical or subtropical, so fruits produced are mostly tropical fruits, such as mango, coconuts, durian, litchi, sugar cane, jackfruit and so on. The time of Water-Splashing Festival is the ripening season for watermelons, bananas and pineapples. At the village of Kandi, Yongkang Township, Yongde County, LinCang City, one or two days before the Water-Splashing Festival, the village head will take along a few villagers, drive a tractor to the villagers' fields to collect watermelons or bananas. The village head will convene a meeting of the villagers, telling them that the Water-Splashing Festival is coming, and we need every household to donate several watermelons and a few jins (one jin equals to 1/2 kilogram) of bananas to welcome the faraway guests to attend our festival. Then at the appointed time, the village head will go together with some villagers to collect watermelons from every household's watermelon field and bananas in the banana field. Generally, what they collect are the bigger fruits that villagers have picked out themselves. The villagers are willing to donate better fruits in order to make the friends participating in their festival feel their goodwill. The village head drives a tractor full of a variety of fruits back to the village temple, and put the fruits there, waiting for the day of Water-Splashing Festival to ask the foreign tourists and the villagers to taste for free. On the day of Water-Splashing Festival, watermelons are cut into pieces with rinds and put in clean plates, and bananas are also put in plates. All fruits will be put in the shade of the temple, and when people feel tired splashing water, they will run there to taste these delicious fruits.

Delicious "Baba"

Baba is a daily food favored by different ethnic groups in Yunnan. They cook Baba differently in making skills, eating methods and uses. One week or two weeks before the Water-Splashing Festival, Dai women will hurry to cook a lot of "Baba", including "plantain leaves Baba", "glutinous rice Baba", "wind-blow Baba", "glutinous rice grain Baba" and so on. In addition to be taken to the temple for "Danfo" (that is, dedicated to the Lord Buddha) on the day of the Water-Splashing Festival, these "Baba" are also for the whole family's consumption. Because Dai people like glutinous rice, naturally they also like all kinds of snacks made of glutinous rice. Every Water-Splashing Festival, Dai people will make a lot of glutinous rice snacks, one reason of which is that their consumption demand is big, and the other reason is that these Dai "Baba" are also popular in other participating ethnic groups. On the day of Water-Splashing Festival, some women will sell these "Baba" next to the temple or in the bazaar. Tourists come to Dai villages to experience the fun of splashing water, and at the same time they will taste the delicious food of Dai people. Some people will also take the food back to their families. During the Water-Splashing Festival every year, women who sell "Dai Baba" will get a handsome income.

The word "haomen" is Dai language, meaning "plantain leaf Baba"; as the name suggests, it is glutinous rice Baba wrapped in plantain leaves. The raw materials and ingredients needed for making are light green plantain leaves, white glutinous rice, brown sugar, gauze, stone mill and so on. First, soak the clean glutinous rice in clear water for about 3 hours, and then grind the soaked raw glutinous rice into fine rice flour. Now, with the development of science and technology, the tradition of handgrinding has been replaced by rice-grinding machines. What is ground out is raw rice flour with water. Therefore, it is necessary to drain the water with gauze and then put the drained rice flour in a basin and mix well with the crushed brown sugar. The amount of brown sugar is added according to people's taste and preference. Finally, wrap adequate amount of raw rice flour mixed with sugar with plantain leaves into the shape of a cuboid, and steam in the steamer for 2 hours. After they are out, people can taste the hot plantain leaf Baba full of the aroma of plantain leaves, brown sugar and glutinous rice. It is widely popular among Dai people not only because it tastes sweet and delicious, but also because this Baba can be eaten both hot and cold, does not need to be reprocessed, and does not have to dip in other things for it itself has brown sugar.

"Haobeng"means glutinous rice Baba, which Dai people usually pound during the Water-Splashing Festival or the Spring Festival. Different from plantain leaf Baba, glutinous rice Baba is to pound the steamed glutinous rice first, then stick on plantain leaves or flat plastic film, dry in the air and cool off, and then eat by roasting on coals, usually by dipping sesame, honey, white sugar or brown sugar.

The "wind-blow Baba" has its name, according to Dai people, because this kind of Baba is very thin and very light, easily broken with a bite, and will also melt in the mouth. People will become light as a swallow after eating it, and will also feel like a gust of wind blowing. Besides, during the Water-Splashing Festival, there is usually wind blowing, which is usually called by Dai people "New Year wind", and so this kind of food is called "wind-blow Baba".

The "rice grain Baba" is made by directly pressing the steamed glutinous rice gently into small round cakes of about 5 cm in diameter, then putting on a clean mat, drying under the sun before soaking in cooked sweet water, taking out for drying again, and finally deepfrying the dried Baba to turn golden before eating. Deep-fried "rice grain Baba" is crisp and sweet, presented as glutinous rice cake of grains, and so it is called "rice grain Baba".

Waterless rice noodles is the traditional food of Dai people in Dehong, which is indispensable during the festival. When making it, grind the rice, boil it, and grind again, and the rice can be glutinous rice or common rice. It's just that it should end up with a machine milling the rice into a big sheet, and then roll up. Transect the roll of waterless rice noodles into about 5cm wide, shake out to be in threadiness. After being boilt in the pot, put them in the prepared broth and they can be served with seasoning. But waterless rice noodles offered as vegetarian meals are free of oil, with only boiling water and a little brown sugar.

8. The Authentic "*Ganbai*"

The trade fair is a place of leisure, entertainment and consumption for both urban and rural areas. The trade fair in the Water-Splashing Festival is manifesting everywhere the authentic and unique culture of a nation. "*Ganbai*" is the general term of Dai festivals, also called "Zuobai". In fact,

"*Ganbai*" of Dai people covers far more extensively than the trade fair; it is a folk party combining sacrifice, gathering, arts and trade. Though Dai festivals are various, they are generally called "bai", such as Baishuangnan (Water-Splashing Festival), Baiganduo, Baipala, Bailaluo, Baihanshang, Baizang, Baizhai and so on. And participating in these activities is called *Ganbai*.

In 1940, an anthropologist called Tian Rukang did a ten-month field investigation at Namu Village in Mangshi, Yunnan Province. He wrote in his *Bai of Border Inhabitants in Mangshi*, "Bai is a kind of religious ceremony, but the ceremony is associated with the whole life of Baiyi (Dai nationality). Like the so-called inserting Buddha's mountain into a mustard seed in Vimalakirti Sutra, a small religious ceremony should hold the full impact of the whole Dai culture, and even enlighten us to produce a new view for many economic, social and political issues of modern society." In this book, Mr. Tian introduces Dai people's Buddhist worship ceremony at different age stages, the types of bai and ritual process. With the passage of time, some changes have taken place, but *Ganbai* is still the most distinctive feature of the Water-Splashing Festival.

At the time of *Ganbai*, the villagers will gather together at the Buddhist temple to chant sutras, where men beat drums and gongs to greet the Buddha statue. As soon as the Buddha statue arrives, women in splendid constumes will immediately offer flowers and fruits, burn incense and candles. During the festival, people often sing Dai operas or perform other performances and conduct recreational activities. Unmarried young men and women take advantage of this opportunity to pay court to each other and find the right person. On the day, the master of "Zuo bai" will also feast people. According to the traditional custom, doing "Zuobai" once will promote one's religious status to "Tan", twice to"Paga", three times to "Pagale", four times to "Pagalexiang". The higher their religious status is, the more respect they get from the villagers; so the folk custom of Zuobai continues.

As the saying goes, "When the rice turns gold, Dai people will be wild." It is the time of golden rice and the season of harvest, and also the busiest time of "Baiganduo". The time length of "Baiganduo" varies from place to place depending on the large influencial Buddhist temple. Generally, there will be one bai for each Buddhist temple. For example, there are seven large Buddhist temples in Mangshi: Fengping, Jianshan, Guangmu, Mangxing, Zangxiang, Zangmao, Zanghan, so "bai" in Mangshiwill last for seven days, while *Ganbai* in Ruili, Yingjiang, Longchuan and Lianghe lasts three to five days. Bai field is usually arranged in the spacious place near the Buddhist temples, where food, stalls, Achang knife famous inside and outside the province, tobacco of Husaand Nongdao abound. There are also Tongpa (satchel), silver jewellery and soft waterless rice noodles with unique Dai style.

When *Ganbai* is on, people dress up in festive costumes and raise offerings high. The procession is in great force, flocking towards the bai field. The brightly colored costumes, the swaying floral straight dresses, and the beloved companions, all flock to the crowd, enjoying the peacock dance and watching Dai operas. The first sight when entering the fair is the busy figure of Dai women, with the traditional shoulder pole carrying a small bamboo basket. Look by standing on a high place: old men go into Buddhist temple to burn incense and worship the Lord Buddha, praying for children and for making a fortune, and for peace and helath; the middle-aged men are playing the game of elephant-foot drums, dancing the peacock dance and performing Dai plays; young men and women are whispering under the floral umbrellas, and some even go out into the wild to enjoy their romance. Numerous floral umbrellas move towards the depths of the bamboo forest, silently proclaiming the end of the day's *Ganbai*. The next day, people will go to other bai fileds to watch the fun.

The *Ganbai* fair near the Water-Splashing Festival center is generally engaged in snacks, such as stewing sour bamboo shoots with fish, stewing sour bamboo shoots with cured beef, lemon chicken salad, glutinous rice Baba, barbecue, and a variety of fresh fruits and so on. And there are also national costumes, poultry, and native products. Foreign merchants, however, manage clothing, shoes and hats, stationery, toys, audio and video products, electronic products, and production tools, agricultural and sideline products, vegetables, fruit, and even a variety of entertainment items. Large and small stalls, various goods, numerous merchants gathering from different places, tourists coming back and forth, the whole scene is bustling with noise and excitement.

Because of the wide spread of the Water-Splashing Festival, there are more and more tourists, scholars and photographers attracted from other places. The trade fairs of the Water-Splashing Festival not only meet people's needs of goods transaction and consumption; more importantly, they also bear the function of cultural communication, and become a space for the flow of different cultures. In the trade fairs, people can fully appreciate the diverse customs of local ethnic groups, including clothing, cuisine custom, etiquette and custom, and art custom, and for this reason, *Ganbai* has become a concentrated national culture fair.

Tips for Tourism

"*Ganbai*" in Xishuangbanna

Ganbai is a traditional activity of Dai people, which covers actually much more extensively than village fairs. The largest *Ganbai* field in Xishuangbanna is located in the *Ganbai* street of Gaozhuangxishuangjing, Jinghong City, which is a collection of southeast Asian folk culture and artists, specialty snacks, crafts and native products. In addition, during the Water-Splashing Festival, *Ganbai* will also be held by the Lancang River and in Manting Park. *Ganbai* by the Lancang River is on the bare sandbeach, while *Ganbai* activities in Manting Park mainly include strolling in the park and watching dancing performances.

Matters needing attention:

It's very hot in Xishuangbanna, so it is necessary to bring enough T-shirts and shorts, and a thin coat as well. In addition, sunglasses, sunscreen, anti-heatstroke drugs (such as Huangxiangzhengqi capsules) are essential when attending *Ganbai*.

Best travel time:

November to May is the dry season with cool weather, and is the peak season for tourism. Especially in April, for the grand Water-Splashing Festival, the scale of *Ganbai* is especially big.

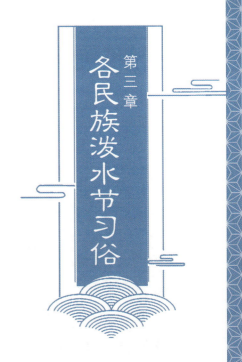

第三章

各民族泼水节习俗

泼水节是中国西南地区的傣、布朗、德昂、阿昌等民族的传统节日，因为涉及面广而得以广泛流布。泼水节是傣族的傣历新年，所以格外受到该民族的重视。同时，泼水节也几乎覆盖了所有信仰南传上座部佛教民族聚居的地方。

一 泼水节在中国的流布

按照参与的人数和规模来看，泼水节主要分布在云南西双版纳傣族自治州、德宏傣族景颇族自治州、孟连傣族拉祜族佤族自治县、耿马傣族佤族自治县、元江哈尼族彝族傣族自治县、新平彝族傣族自治县等地区。

西双版纳

西双版纳傣族自治州是云南省成立的第一个少数民族自治州，位于云南省最南端。西双版纳是国家级生态示范区和国家级风景名胜区，具有"热带雨林、避寒胜地、和谐家园、神秘风情"等自然与人文特色相结合的风貌，是"东南亚傣民族寻根的好地方、北方人避寒过冬的好地方、国内外游客亲近自然追求健康的好地方"。这里以神奇的热带雨林自然景观和少数民族风情而闻名于世，是中国热门旅游景点之一。

每年公历4月13～15日的西双版纳泼水节最富盛名，被誉为"东方狂欢节"。

○森林公园欢庆泼水节（云南勐腊）

旅游小贴士

西双版纳景洪

景洪是西双版纳傣族自治州首府，位于云南南部，西双版纳傣族自治州中部。素有"东方多瑙河"之称的澜沧江—湄公河穿流而过，是中国进入东南亚各国的主要通道。这座旅游边城，民族风情浓郁，亚热带风光迷人。市中心有秀丽的孔雀湖，湖面倒映着街道两旁挺拔的油棕、贝叶、槟榔、椰子。

著名景点：

西双版纳森林公园、热带植物园、傣族园、野象谷、勐泐大佛寺等。

最佳旅游时间：

每年11月至次年4月，气温较为舒适，不冷不热。

德宏

德宏傣族景颇族自治州地处中国西南边陲，"德宏"是傣语的音译，"德"为下面，"宏"为怒江，意思是："怒江下游的地方"。德宏民族众多，节日丰富。包括傣族、阿昌族的泼水节、景颇族的目瑙纵歌节、阿昌族的阿露窝罗节等，其中泼水节最为盛大和有名。

○壮斋泼水节（云南瑞丽）

旅游小贴士

德宏瑞丽

瑞丽是古代南方丝路的重要通道，是中缅两国贸易的中转站和集散地。瑞丽市地处云南省西南部，隶属于德宏傣族景颇族自治州。陆路距州府芒市 99 千米，距省会昆明 890 千米，是起于上海的 320 国道的终点，是昆瑞公路与史迪威公路的交汇处。其西北、西南、东南三面与缅甸山水相连、村寨相依。现辖姐告边境贸易区、畹町经济开发区两区，勐卯镇、畹町镇、弄岛镇三镇，以及姐相乡、户育乡、勐秀乡三个乡。

注意事项：

瑞丽紫外线较强，外出需要注意防晒，建议准备好遮阳伞、太阳镜、帽子、防晒霜。7~9 月份来瑞丽，可穿短袖、裙子，也可以带一件薄衫。

最佳旅游时间：

瑞丽的最佳旅游时间为 7-9 中旬。

瑞丽属南亚热带季风性气候，全年分旱雨两季，年平均气温在 21℃左右，没有雪天，冬天也不会很冷，夏天很热，鲜花四季常开。

普洱市

普洱市别称思茅，是云南省的一个地级市，位于云南省西南部。泼水节在普洱市的主要流布地为景谷傣族彝族自治县和孟连傣族拉祜族佤族自治县。

111

旅游小贴士

普洱思茅

思茅区，隶属于普洱市，位于云南省南部、普洱市中南部、澜沧江中下游。思茅区是普洱市委、政府所在地，是普洱市的政治、经济、文化中心和连接东南亚的交通枢纽。思茅区是历史上的茶马古道——南方丝绸之路的起点，为云南三大海关重镇之一，曾有"东南亚陆路码头"和"银思茅"之称。

著名景点：

思茅区的主要遗迹有石屏会馆、思茅文庙、思茅老海关、茶马古道、茶城观景台等。

思茅的茶城观景台建设以原始生态环境为基础，不破坏周围茶树林，稍加人工雕凿而成，把观景台带入茶林中，为公众提供一个以休闲为主的场所。在观景台，西北面近看连绵起伏的茶地，远处眺望美丽的中国茶城；西南面可观赏自然生态茶山、湖泊干海子和风景名胜区梅子湖公园，湖边群山环抱；远处是一望无际的思茅松。到此观景，心旷神怡。著名的茶马古道沿途高山逶迤，峡谷纵横，风光旖旎，气候多变，民风古朴，令人惊叹她曾经见证过普洱茶贸易的盛衰，是博大精深的普洱茶文化的重要载体。

最佳旅游时间：

四季皆宜。

临沧和玉溪

　　泼水节在临沧市的主要流布地为耿马傣族佤族自治县和双江拉祜族佤族布朗族傣族自治县；在玉溪市的主要流布地为元江哈尼族彝族傣族自治县和新平彝族傣族自治县。

○花腰傣的泼水欢歌（云南新平）

旅游小贴士

花　腰　傣

　　花腰傣是人们对居住在红河中上游新平、元江两县的傣族的一种称谓。因其服饰古朴典雅、雍容华贵，特别是服饰的腰部彩带层层束腰，绣有绚丽斑斓的精美图案，挂满艳丽闪亮的缨穗、银泡、银铃而称为"花腰傣"。花腰傣的名称最早见于清朝，居住在红河

113

中游的傣族为"花摆夷"。花腰傣是民国时期其他民族对傣族的称呼。花腰傣由傣雅、傣洒、傣卡三个支系组成。不仅在服饰文化上与滇南的傣泐、滇西的傣那显著不同，而且这里的傣族不信佛教，没有文字，不过泼水节，保留着中国傣族在未接受印度佛教文化影响之前原有的文化状况。

在新平嘎洒、水塘两个乡镇的花腰傣自称傣洒，新平腰街镇和元江县甘庄镇的自称傣卡，新平县漠沙镇、元江县东峨乡的自称傣雅。花街节（也称"赶花节"）是傣族青年男女相互认识、谈情说爱、挑选伴侣的盛大节日。花腰傣的竹编、篾帽、腰萝、银饰、制陶等久负盛名。

注意事项：

花腰傣主人将菜夹给客人时，不能推让或转夹给别人。主人斟酒时也不要推让，喝不完剩下即可。花腰傣有嚼槟榔的习惯，因此见到她们大多数牙齿发黑，她们在一定程度上也会以此为美。

著名景点：

新平——哀牢山自然保护区、磨盘山国家森林公园、新化古州野林、杨武温泉等。

元江——元江哀牢梯田、彩色膏林、妙莲寺、那诺哈尼云海梯田等。

最佳旅游时间：

夏秋两季最佳，特别是在农历五月初六前后，可以赶上花腰傣盛大的花街节。

其他地区

除了大部分傣族聚集的自治州、自治县存在大规模的泼水节活动以外，由于泼水节对于德昂族、布朗族、阿昌族等民族民众而言也是一年一度的欢乐盛会，因此在这些民族聚集的相关地域，也有着相应的分布与传播。

德昂族主要分布在德宏的芒市、瑞丽（含畹町经济区）、陇川、盈江、梁河等县市，保山市隆阳区和临沧市的镇康、耿马、永德等县及思茅市的澜沧县也有少量分布。中缅边境一线德宏段周围均有德昂族聚居区，被德昂族称为"浇花节"的泼水节分布在德宏州梁河县河西乡二古城村、芒市三台山乡初冬瓜村及邦外村、芒市五岔路乡、芒市镇和瑞丽市雷闷村、临沧市镇康县等地方。

过泼水节的布朗族主要分布在西双版纳州的勐海县、景洪市、勐腊县，普洱市的思茅区、澜沧县、景谷县，临沧市的双江县、耿马县、镇康县、永德县。在上述县级行政区域中，布朗族人口最多的是双江拉祜族佤族布朗族傣族自治县和勐海县，过泼水节的人也最集中。双江县只有如邦丙乡的令地村不信佛、不过此节，其余全过。西双版纳州的景洪市以北的布朗族、勐腊县的布朗族克木人不过此节。普洱市澜沧县的布朗族基本全过。思茅区、景谷县的布朗族都过。

阿昌族是云南人口较少的 8 个世居民族之一，主要分布在德宏州陇川县的户撒和梁河县的囊宋、九保三个民族乡，其他分布在芒市、保山市龙陵县、腾冲县及大理州的云龙县境内。阿昌族也是一个跨境民族，在缅甸，被称为"迈达"族，人口约 4 万人，主要分布在克钦邦的密支那及掸邦的南欧、景栋等地。

除了西南少数民族地区，如今泼水节随着人口的迁移、文化的传播，在深圳锦绣中华民俗村、北京中华民族园等旅游景点，每年的五六月间也会举办表演性更强的泼水节，吸引游客参与体验傣族文化。

○节日中的哈尼族（僾尼人）少女（云南勐腊）

而在福建省石狮市，还有另外一种"海上泼水节"，它是石狮蚶江两岸福建、台湾的汉族传统民俗节日。农历五月初五端午节，俗称"五月节"，是汉族最古老的传统节日之一。中原汉人南徙，带来了中原纪念屈原的端午风俗。据传说，屈原投江后，当时楚人因舍不得贤臣屈原死去，于是有许多人划船追赶营救。他们争先恐后，追至洞庭湖时不见踪迹，是为龙舟竞渡之起源，后每年五月五日划龙舟以纪念之。而这一天，两岸对渡的船只都要在蚶江海边追逐泼水，以这种欢快的方式互祝吉祥、交融情谊，并祈求平安兴旺。"海上泼水"的习俗由此产生并代代相传，传承了300多年，成为一种别具特色的闽台对渡文化习俗，也是全球仅有的"海上泼水节"习俗。美丽的西双版纳与美丽的蚶江，不同的地点、不同的民族，一样的民俗、一样的情感。

二
傣族的泼水节

　　傣族是云南省的特有民族之一，在各种书画与影视作品中，那身着艳丽筒裙的傣女，总是以水样的灵动与秀美呈现在世人面前。电影《孔雀公主》早已成为美丽与神奇的代名词；舞蹈家刀美兰的《水》，杨丽萍的《孔雀公主》和《雀之灵》，让人怦然心动；画家袁熙坤在首都机场的那幅《生命之水》曾经引起巨大轰动，而丁绍光的浓墨重彩画，更是将傣女的美演绎得无以复加。在人们的印象中，每每看到傣女，总会想起《红楼梦》中贾宝玉所说："女儿家是水做的骨肉。"这句话用在傣女身上，应该最恰当不过。其实，对傣族更多些了解后会发现，不独傣族女性是"水做的骨肉"，连傣族男子也被称为"水的儿子"，傣语叫"鲁傣鲁喃"。傣族是"一个水的民族"，他们临水而居，喜水、爱水又崇水，更是围绕着"水"这一因子，创造出了独特的水文化，构成了傣族文化中最重要的一部分。所以有人说："傣族像水，她能够约束自己，流过峡谷浅溪，也能够汇成汪洋，一泻千里；她还善于反映自己的颜色，当其天空是蓝色，她便是蓝色，当其天空是红色，她便是红色，然而她便是她，她纯净而无色。"斗转星移，春华秋实，寒来暑往，在傣家人心中，水早已不是简单的物质实体，而是浸润着傣族一年又一年光景的神秘力量。居住于水乡泽国的傣族及其先民们，日日与水相生相息，而作为傣族与水关系最密切的节日——泼水节，更是集中蕴含了傣族人的精神思考和思维理念，深刻体现着傣族人民的价值观念、审美情趣，因其而创造出来的文化艺术具有独特的民族特征与地方特性。

泼水节对于傣族而言，这个最隆重的节日实际上是他们的新年，时间大约在公历的 4 月 13 日至 4 月 15 日之间，一般持续 3 ~ 7 天。泼水节，傣语称"桑罕比迈"，是傣族人民辞旧迎新的传统节日。节日的第一天为除夕，傣语叫做"宛多尚罕"，意思是送旧；第二天叫"宛脑"，意思是空日，即这一天既不列入旧年也不属于新年；第三天为元旦，称"宛叭宛玛"，即"日子之王到来的一天"。泼水节这几天，村村寨寨的傣族群众都沉浸在喜气洋洋的欢乐气氛之中。泼水节的第一天，有些临江的寨子会赛龙舟，澜沧江边的傣族村寨尤为热闹，成千上万的傣族群众从四面八方聚集到澜沧江边观看龙船比赛。在除夕和元旦之间的空日里，傣族群众身着盛装赶到各寨去参加大型的赶摆活动，男女青年在广场上兴致勃勃地玩丢包游戏，寻找自己的意中人。"包"一般为 4 ~ 5 寸的正方形，用各种不同颜色的布缝制而成，内装棉花籽、攀枝花籽或者粗糠，四角饰以彩色布条，上钉一根布带作为丢包绳。当夕阳西下，姑娘们成群赶到寨边空旷场地时，小伙子们早已等候在那里站成一排。姑娘们走来与小伙子相距约 20 米左右，把鲜花抛给他们作赠品，表示丢包开始。而赶摆场的另一角会燃放起高升，随着人们的一阵阵欢呼声，高升在空中绽放开。晚上，人们燃放起孔明灯，把夜空点缀得多姿多彩。到了元旦这天，男女老少沐浴更衣，青年男女更是精心打扮，他们穿上最漂亮的衣服，戴上最喜爱的首饰和鲜花。清晨，人们抬着供品到佛寺赕佛，每一户人家都在佛寺旁用沙子堆成四五尺高的沙塔，插上

泼水节

鲜花和彩纸，并在沙塔旁聆听佛爷诵经，之后举行浴佛礼。浴佛之后，狂欢活动——泼水便迫不及待地开始了。

○傣家喜迎节日（云南盈江）

三

德昂族的泼水节

德昂族主要聚居于云南省德宏傣族景颇族自治州，有本民族语言，多使用傣文。

四月，中国的北方刚卸去银装，冬寒未尽，而在孔雀之乡——

○村寨中的德昂族泼水节（云南芒市）

德宏却早已百花盛开，春意盎然。德昂族的泼水节恰在这个鸟语花香的季节悄然来临。每年清明节后的第七天，树木和竹林环绕的德昂族村寨便沸腾了。身着绣有鲜艳图案的花格筒裙、钉着银扣紧身衣的德昂族姑娘，背起了装有竹水筒的竹篮去过泼水节了。泼水节本为傣历新年的庆祝活动，德昂族因为信仰南传上座部佛教，因此也同样以泼水节的形式来庆祝新年的到来。德昂族的泼水节叫"浇花节"，目前已列入国家级非物质文化遗产保护名录。但在民间，该节日在德昂族内部还未形成统一称呼。虽然总体上或称泼水节或称浇花节，但不同支系的名称并不相同："绕买"支系称为"浴佛节"，"布列"支系称为"洪普腊"，"梁"支系称做"尚建"，皆是浴佛的意思。浇花节，德昂语称为"库户波桑建"。"库户波"，德昂语意为"浇花"；"桑建"，源于印度梵语，指"浴佛节"。尽管浇花节在国家非物质文化遗产名录中得到认定，但许多德昂族特别是散杂居地区的德昂族仍习惯称泼水节，或将泼水节与浇花节二者糅合在一起，也仍按照传统的方式来庆祝这一节日。

德昂族过浇花节的时间约在公历的四月中旬。与傣族的泼水节习俗相比较，德昂族的浇花节不仅是"浴佛节"，还是"缅怀和崇拜母亲的节日"。届时，每家的晚辈要准备一盆热水，端来放在堂屋中央，把家里的父母等长辈请出来坐在堂上，向他们叩头请罪，请他们原谅晚辈一年来不孝顺的地方。长辈们也要检讨一年来在为晚辈树立榜样方面做得不足的地方。然后，晚辈为长辈洗手洗脚，同时互祝来年在和睦、勤劳的气氛中度过。如果父母去世，兄长、姐姐和嫂嫂、姐夫就成为洗手洗脚的对象。关于这个独特的敬老习俗，流传较广的主要有两个传说。

第一个传说是一个悲伤的故事。相传很久以前，一位德昂族寡妇省吃俭用，当她辛辛苦苦把儿子抚养成人时，已累瞎了眼睛。儿子见妈妈做活不如以前了，非常不满，经常骂她。有一年清明节的第七天，儿子上山干活，看见一只羽毛未丰满的小乌鸦，来来回回找虫子喂一只又老又瘦的乌鸦，此情此景感化了儿子，他骂自己不如"含食报娘恩"的小乌鸦，决心好好服侍妈妈。就在这时，又病又饿的妈妈摸着路给儿子送饭来了，她一阵头昏跌倒在半路上。当凉风把她吹醒时，想到儿子一定饿极了，就连忙挣扎着往山上爬，爬着爬着，她听到儿子从山上跑下来的脚步声。妈妈怕挨骂，心一横撞死在路旁的大树上。儿子是来向妈妈认错的，见妈妈被他吓死了，哭得死去活来，痛悔莫及。儿子把妈妈埋葬后，把树砍下来雕成一尊母亲塑像供在家里。从此，每年清明后第七天儿子都会上山采来锥栗树花枝，蘸着竹筒里从山沟中背来的清水，把塑像浸到洒着花瓣的温水中清洗。以后就演变为一种习俗，从此，德昂族就有了竹篮背水，用花枝蘸水相互洒，并为老人洗手洗脚的泼水节。

第二个传说来源于一个更为神秘和古老的神话。古时候，开天避地的万能佛祖，为了帮助德昂人民料理生产生活大事，经过天神同意，从天上来到人间。为了不引起人们的大惊小怪，佛祖下凡后，变成了一个佛爷，独自住在奘房里。他为人民办了很多好事，解脱了不少灾难，深得百姓们的敬重和爱戴。大家有什么疑难都来找他帮助解决。最初，百姓们只是遇到喜、丧、住、食等事情时才找他解决。因为他是智慧的化身，办法很多，什么问题都解决得恰到好处。久而久之，连哪块田种什么庄稼，哪个小伙子娶什么样的姑娘，哪个小孩取什么样的名子，哪个老人有多长寿命等大小事情，都来向他求教。有时，夫妻稍不和睦，也要找他调解，弄得他昼夜不得安宁。他逐步感到人间的事情太多、太杂，但是想到勤劳善良的德昂族人民，他又舍不得离开人间。天神答应他下凡的时间满了，三番五次地催他返回天宫。佛祖虽然留恋德昂族人民，又不敢对抗天神，急得害了大病，卧床不起。百姓知道了，到四面八方找来名贵药材，敬献给他用。佛祖知道天神要召他的魂上天，吃药也无济于事。一天，他的病情突然恶化，男女老少都跑来问他有什么要求。他只要求人们按他的相貌雕一个木像，再为他洗一个澡。百姓们就照着做，三天后，佛像的轮廓雕出来了。佛爷睁开眼睛看看，点点头，满意地说："万事顺心。"说完就闭上了眼睛。半月后，佛像的脚手雕成了，佛爷睁开眼看看，微笑着说："风调雨顺收成好。"说完又闭上眼睛。过了一个月，佛像的眼、耳、口、鼻全部雕成了。这时清明已过，佛爷睁大眼睛，对着佛像看了又看，十分高兴地说："魔鬼避开，人畜无病。"谁知，百姓来不及帮他洗澡，他就离开了人间。为了表示对他的怀念，也为了完成他的嘱咐，百姓们照着奘房的式样，就地盖起了风格别致的凉亭，将佛像置于亭子正中，并且赶了3天大摆，给佛像泼了3天的水。自此以后，德昂族年年都要泼水，便逐渐形成了节日，叫做"散根"，意为泼水节。

　　这两个传说一直流传下来。随着社会的不断发展，德昂族又为泼水节赋予了新的内容。节日里，人们不仅要穿上节日的盛装，首先给佛爷、佛像浇水，以示对祖先、恩人的怀念和敬重；然后为年过六旬的长寿老人洗尘拜寿，表示对他们的感谢和祝愿。这些仪式结束后，青年男女便相互泼水，特别是向新婚的夫妇泼水道喜，祝愿他们和睦相处，一辈子幸福。

　　德昂族泼水节与傣族的泼水节既相似又不同。临近节日，人们忙着缝制新衣，做米粑，制作水龙、水桶等泼水工具。节日第一天清晨，信众们便从家里携带事先准备好的各种供品前来奘房赕佛。进入奘房以后即把供品赕给佛爷。佛爷要向信众念一段"芒格拉"（祝福语），大概内容是："感谢你送给我吃的、用的，我祝你祖祖辈辈都有吃有穿，祝你一家身体健康，万事如意，明年比今年更好。"

　　赕佛仪式结束后。佛爷开始请佛，前来奘房的信众皆双手合十，虔诚地跪在奘房内的地板上，聆听佛爷诵经：

　　尊敬的佛祖，今天我们过节，我带着我们各家各户来请示佛。我们要请佛出来住，要给你洗浴干净，希望你更好看些，希望佛能体谅我们的善心。过去一年我们有什么不对的地方，向佛请示，希望佛原谅我们。在一年当中，希望佛保佑我们更顺利，和平幸福，幸福美好。

　　当佛爷诵完这段经文以后，信众们在佛爷的带领下开始齐声念诵道：

　　尊敬的佛祖，我笃信这样的佛教。同时，我要求自己不再去偷、抢、打、骂别人，不做下流的事情。我会好好地信它，它会带我们过上幸福的生活，它会让我的心走向正直的道路。我信奉佛教，会尊重老人、爱护儿女、拥护民族。我们要听佛爷的话，听老人的话，不参加不愉快的活动，不要有打架斗殴的事。要尊重父母，爱护民族。父母教育我们不要去偷东西，不去做坏事，不抢别人的东西，更不要去做恶劣的事。不管我们遇到什么民族，包括国外的那些民族，我们都是亲戚朋友，要团结一致，只有这样我们才能和睦相处，共同发展。这些是祖祖辈辈传下来的，让我们这样去相信的。

○德昂族泼水节中的祭祀（云南芒市）

　　以上诵经大约持续半个小时。之后人们把佛像从奘房请到竜亭放置好，便开始了滴水仪式：往地上滴清净之水。同时念诵如下经文："各路神仙，我们已经用水来供奉过你了，给你施过功德了。请求你帮我记住我的过失和德行，同时保佑我们不要再去闯祸，不要让我们去犯同样的错误。"

　　之后，便有姑娘提桶端盆，端着吉祥之水，为佛洗尘。浴佛前，佛爷还要带领村民诵一段经文，大意是："尊敬的佛祖，我们已经把你请出来了，在以后的几天里我们会每天用清水来洗浴你，希望你干干净净的。请佛保佑我们也干干净净的。"人们通过浴佛，用清净向佛表达诚意，同时也希望佛回馈给自己清净。

　　这时，德高望重的长者便手持鲜花，蘸水轻轻地洒向周围的人群，向大家祝福，祝贺新年的开始。人们开始兴奋起来，纷纷互相祝贺新年。年轻人将水桶高高举过头顶，将水滴洒在老年人的手上，祝愿他们生活快乐、健康长寿。老人们则伸出双手，将水棒在手中，口念祝词，为年轻人道喜、祝福。仪式结束之后，人们便以象脚鼓为前导，排成长队，拥向泉边、河畔，唱歌、跳舞，互相追逐、泼水。

泼水节既是德昂族人民欢度新年的典礼,又是男女青年谈情说爱、寻找心上人的好时机。德昂族流行一种赠竹篮习俗。清明节快到时,小伙子磨快长刀,砍来最好的竹子编制竹篮。泼水节的前三天,小伙子把篮子精心编好,乘夜深人静"串姑娘"时,将篮子分别送给所有来参与的姑娘。其中最漂亮的那只,要送给自己最喜爱的姑娘,以此表达自己的爱意,试探对方的反应。此时,每个姑娘往往都能收到好几个竹篮,然而姑娘究竟钟情于谁呢?这就要看泼水节那天姑娘背的是谁送她的那只竹篮了。到了这一天,姑娘们人人都背上了一个精致美观的竹篮,但究竟是谁的呢?这下可忙坏了小伙子们,他们睁圆双眼,紧盯着姑娘们身上的竹篮,仔细辨认着心上人所背的是否是自己送给她的那只竹篮。对对情人相遇后,便互相尽情地泼水、嬉戏,以表达自己激动、喜悦的心情。这个时候,竹篮便不仅是传情的信物,也成了泼水节少不了的工具。

节日的早上,小伙子陪着身背竹篮的姑娘排成长队,敲着象脚鼓到井边、沟里背清水,然后回到寨子边的寺庙。这时成年男子拿出最大的铓、最大的镲,在象脚鼓的伴奏下跳起了铓镲舞。边跳边带领男女老少围着寺庙转,转了四五圈后,停下舞蹈。大家围在喷水的彩龙周围,姑娘们依次登上高高屹立在彩龙旁的木架上,拿出斜背在身子一侧的竹篮里的竹筒,把清水倒进龙身。彩龙立刻喷珠吐玉,欢呼的人们手舞足蹈,象脚鼓越敲越响,泼水节开始了。

未婚的男女,有的抱着竹筒,有的抬着口缸,从竹筒里、口缸中拿出一束淡黄色的锥栗树花,将水轻轻地互相洒在肩上,相互祝福,迎接新的一年到来。节日中一泼就是三天。各家背着清水,将竹筒举起,把水泼在老人的手上,祝愿老人长命百岁,然后帮老人洗脸洗手。再背着水到其他家去,帮各家老人洗脸洗手,请老人吃泼水粑粑。直到全寨子的老人都吃过泼水粑粑,泼水节也就在敬老活动中结束了。需要强调的是，德昂族的泼水方式有一定规范。例如，给老人浇水时，只能用盛着清泉水的小竹水筒，且要插上花，让水顺着花束滴到老人伸出的手心上，不能泼到身上。男女青年之间相互泼水时，也必须用竹筒，轻轻地从肩膀往下泼，不能泼在头上。未婚男女青年在给新婚夫妇泼水时，相互间都不准出现不礼貌的粗野行为。不然，轻则受到众人斥责，重则被剥夺参加泼水节的权利。

四
阿昌族的泼水节

居住在云南省德宏州陇川、梁河等县的阿昌族，是一个人口只有2万多人的民族，全国为云南所特有，属于跨境而居的少数民族。阿昌族与傣族、景颇族、傈僳族等民族杂居，在生活、文化各方面都受傣族影响较大。

阿昌族的泼水节分为上山采花、赕佛、献佛、沐佛和相互泼水祝福等几个过程。每年清明节后的第七天，是阿昌族泼水节的开端。这天上午，男女老幼穿上节日盛装，采来鲜花，女性插在头上，男性别在胸前。下午四点左右，全寨的中青年男子汇集在佛寺前。两面龙凤旗开路，前面一人舞着户撒刀，后面几人跳着象脚鼓舞，浩浩荡荡，一路鸣枪，向山里进发。上山后，在锥栗树前鸣响鞭炮、跪拜，然后采锥栗树花、杜鹃花。采花毕，人人兴高彩烈，挥舞花枝，纵情歌舞；跳够了阿昌族的民间舞蹈，一路敲着象脚鼓回到村寨。村里的妇女早已准备好苏子粑粑。当听到采花队伍鸣铜炮枪报信时，立刻挑选十来个姑娘端着苏子粑粑往村外迎接。采花的男子向姑娘们献花，姑娘则把一盆盆的苏子粑粑送过去，请采花人吃，然后同歌同舞回村，吃完后一同欢歌纵舞进入村寨。老人们早在佛寺前立起竹竿等待。大家把采来的花一圈一圈地扎在竿上做成花塔；有的村则做成竹轿子样，插上花谓之"花轿"。这时已是夜里十点左右，人们不但不散，反而围着花塔、花轿载歌载舞到深夜。

第二天和第三天，人们开始"浇花水"。男子敲响象脚鼓、钯、镲，扛着四色彩旗在前面开路，姑娘在后排成一长串，到河里挑清水泼花塔、花轿，并把清水倒进竹龙，喷洒花轿里供着的佛。

第四天晚上，小伙子相约去串村。他们刚进这个村，就被村里汇集在一起的姑娘们请到一姑娘家去安睡。姑娘们则到另一姑娘家去，按照来的小伙子人数，一人杀一支鸡，然后，煎、炒、煮、炖，做成八样菜，以她们高超的烹调技术，引起小伙子们的爱慕。到了凌晨两点，一个碗装一个鸡头，一个碗盛满米酒。一双筷子，一人一套摆上圆桌，姑娘才去请小伙子进餐："来串的小伙子啊，我们做了点饭菜，请去尝一尝。"小伙子原本是去"串"的，一来就请去睡觉，岂能睡得着。躺在床上睁着眼睛，竖着耳朵，静候佳音。听到姑娘的声音，又不敢冒失，于是装着不好意思不开腔。姑娘们见没动静，再请一遍，小伙子人才齐声说："我们厚脸皮去吃吧。"大家起来跟着姑娘们走。入席后，互相说些客套话，又是男一句、女一句对歌到天亮。经这样一番接触交往，有情人缔结良缘，歌声于是更为缠绵。小伙子要回村了，临走前，把事先凑好的鸡钱藏在墙缝里或是压在碗下，留给姑娘们去找。然后，各人拿着自己碗里的鸡头告别姑娘。他们

127

也各自通过这一活动，播种下了爱情的种子。

○阿昌族妇女服饰（云南梁河）

○节日中的阿昌族载歌载舞（云南陇川）

户撒阿昌族乡

户撒乡为中国仅有的 3 个阿昌族民族乡之一，位于德宏州陇川县西北部。户撒乡政府驻地姐相村距陇川县政府驻地章凤镇 53 公里，为多民族共居乡，其中阿昌族占多数。

主要特色：

户撒最著名的就是阿昌族的户撒刀锻制技艺，已入选国家级非物质文化遗产保护名录。户撒刀锻制技艺主要集中在潘乐、户早、隆光、相姐、明社、芒炳 6 个村。

最佳旅游时间：

四季皆宜。

五
布朗族的泼水节

泼水节也是布朗族的传统节日，流行于西双版纳州布朗族聚居地区。布朗族全国仅为云南特有，是跨境而居的少数民族。主要聚居在西双版纳州勐海县的布朗山和西定、巴达、打洛山区，其余的散居在临沧、普洱等地。由于居住的地区各异，昔日的布朗人有不同的自称。中华人民共和国成立后，根据本民族意愿，统称为布朗族。

布朗族居住的地区大多在海拔 1500～2300 米的亚热带山区。群山峻岭中密布着参天蔽日的原始森林。这里雨量充沛、四季无霜，盛产桐油树、香樟等经济林木。布朗人以农业为主，种植旱稻、棉花与茶叶，其聚居地是驰名中外的普洱茶原料产地之一。

布朗族的"泼水节"有多种称谓，包括"桑堪节""宋坎节""桑堪比迈节""桑衍节"等。泼水节是布朗族盛大的年节，每逢农历三月清明节后第七日举行，即公历 4 月 13 日到 15 日举行。尽管泼水节有不同的称谓，但都源自南传上座部佛教词语音译，大致包含"敬太阳神""迎接新的收获"和"赕佛"之意。节日里的主要活动是相互泼水以迎接太阳。每年的泼水节前一天，村寨中的青年男女便带着竹盒、竹篮前往河中捞沙，背回缅寺，在缅寺广场前堆沙祭佛。次日，在太阳出山前，就穿戴整齐，手持锥栗花、椿木树枝，齐集村头。青年男子击鼓列队前往缅寺，并把花朵、树条插于沙堆上，

○节日中的布朗族村寨的民间舞蹈（云南双江）

每天插花 3～5 次。还要在村寨东边搭起彩棚，摆上供案，奉上糯米、酒、肉、芭蕉等，由寨老主持送月落、迎日出。人们迎着东方喷薄而出的旭日，载歌载舞，感谢太阳给人间以温暖，给万物以生机。早饭之后，人们结队到佛寺去插花、浴佛，泼水祝福，并堆沙塔、打竹球、载歌载舞、丢包游戏，欢庆新的一天的到来。到了夜间，青年男女尽情欢唱，热闹非凡。现在，节日的内容比过去有很多改变，除以往的传统活动外，又增加了文娱节目的表演和体育比赛，更为人们所欢迎。

○节日中的布朗族舞蹈（云南勐海）

旅游小贴士

普洱茶的故乡：勐海

勐海县位于云南省西南部、西双版纳州西部，东接景洪市，东北接普洱市，西北与澜沧县毗邻，西、南与缅甸接壤。勐海不仅是

131

中国布朗族数量最多的地区之一，还是"普洱茶"的故乡和中国产茶最早之地。境内茶园众多，有1700年前的野生"茶树王"和800余年前的人工栽培型茶树。勐海县民族风情浓郁，傣族的"泼水节"、哈尼族的"嘎汤帕节"、拉祜族的"扩塔节"、布朗族的"桑衎节"集中展示了当地独特的民风民俗文化。

主要景点：

境内的主要景点有景真八角亭、独树成林、打洛森林公园、曼短佛寺、巴达野生茶树王、曼峦回清真寺、勐邦水库等。

最佳旅游时间：

四季皆宜。

六

佤族的泼水节

佤族主要分布在澜沧江以西、萨尔温江以东的怒山山脉南段地区，是滇西南地区古老的少数民族之一，在中国仅云南特有，是跨境而居的少数民族。佤族历史悠久、文化丰富。因支系众多，习俗有所差异。在数量众多的传统节日中，绝大部分与民间信仰有关。但也有部分信仰南传上座部佛教的佤族，文化上受傣族的影响，将泼水节纳入到本民族支系的节日体系中。耿马傣族佤族自治县的勐简大寨的佤族就是典型。这里的佤族属于阿勒佤支系的叶荣谱系，因身穿土黄色的衣服，又被称为"黄衣阿佤"。勐简大寨佤族的节日文化丰富多彩，但和其他居住地的佤族节日存在一定的差别。在众多的节日文化中，泼水节是最为隆重、最有特色、也最能集中体现勐简大寨佤族传统文化的重大节日之一。

勐简大寨佤族泼水节，又称"堆沙节"，是勐简大寨佤族一年中最隆重和盛大的节日，除了水，以"沙"为载体呈现出与其他民族泼水节习俗不同的方面，集中展现了当地的泼水节特色。佤族的泼水节于每年清明节后第四天开始，历时8天。这时，旱季将逝，雨季将临，因此，又是送旧迎新的节日。节日起源于一个传说：

从前有一个人犯了罪，因感罪孽深重，于是天天到深山河流中取回洁净的细沙，在缅寺周围边洒边向佛祖忏悔，祈求得到佛祖的宽恕。佛祖为其改过诚心所动，赦免了他的罪孽，让他重新做人。此后，人们无论有无罪过都会拿沙到缅寺堆放，以求消除罪孽或向佛祖祈福，使自己来年顺顺利利。天长日久，送沙、拿沙、捂沙、堆沙便成为了节日的四大主题，延续至今。

勐简大寨的泼水节由一系列围绕"沙"的仪式所构成。

第一，送沙。所谓送沙，就是村民们将一年来取自深山河流中的干净沙子送到缅寺。勐简大寨佤族认为，沙是最洁净无瑕、能辟邪驱鬼的神物，洒沙奉佛，就能得到佛的保佑和祝福。这种信仰，就使送沙成为了勐简大寨佤族泼水节中历时最长的一项活动，从4月9日一直持续到13日。这5天中，送沙活动一直不停。每天清晨，佛寺里的小和尚都会带领寨里的青年男子击鼓、敲铓，轮流到村寨中心汇合成送沙队伍。村民听到鼓声（或铓声）便换上传统服饰，带上一年来取自深山河流中的干净沙子到广场汇合，然后在小和尚引领下将沙送到缅寺堆沙台里。他们边洒沙边祈祷："请保佑我们顺顺利利，无病无灾，庄稼丰收，养殖兴旺。"洒沙完毕，逐一进入缅寺向佛祖点蜡烛、磕头、祈福。

第二，拿沙。就是到深山河流中取干净的沙，再送到缅寺。这天清晨，村民在佛寺小和尚带领下，跟随击鼓、敲锣队伍前往位于大寨西侧9公里外的老厂河拿沙。老厂河远离村寨，道路坎坷崎岖，那里河水清澈见底，还有两棵千年之久的大青树巍然屹立。勐简大寨佤族视青树为"神树"，对青树的崇拜十分虔诚，因而一年一度的泼水节中，对老厂河青树的祭祀是一项必不可少的活动。村民到达老厂河边后，首先在那里沐浴，然后到老厂河上游，在那个平日里几乎无人进入的地方取洁净的沙子。取沙后，大家围着大青树跳摆欢娱。佛寺和尚在大青树下点燃两根蜡烛，念经祈福。伴随着声声祈福，村民将祈福"花"插在青树周围，完成对老厂河青树的祭献。祭献完毕，大家一路跳摆返回缅寺。回到村寨时，村中年轻人和孩童手提盛水工具，将水泼洒向拿沙归来之人，感谢他们跋山涉水到老厂河拿沙为整个村寨祈福，另一方面也祝福对方吉祥平安。到达缅寺后，他们将自己从老厂河取回的干净沙子边祈福边分洒到四周的堆沙台中。堆沙完毕，人们逐一进入缅寺向佛祖点蜡烛磕头。只有这样，所有愿望方能被佛祖知道，从而得到佛祖的保佑。

第三，捂沙。指停止和沙有关的一切活动，进行洗佛滴水。4月15日这天清晨，村中一部分男子手持葫芦到山中取水，一部分男子则在缅寺前搭建洗佛支架。他们将佛像抬出，放到支架上。支架四周有四个水槽对准佛像，男子从山中取回清水后，爬上高台将水缓缓倒入水槽中，水顺槽而下流到佛像的身上，又汇入佛像下的接水槽中。这时，村民纷纷用接水槽中的水洗脸。他们认为，这水能洗去疾病，带来健康和美丽。洗罢，将水洒向周围的同伴，祝福对方身体健康，万事顺意。待所有洗佛水用完后，佛爷指挥大家将佛像抬回寺中，拆掉洗佛架，等待着村中老人前来滴水。下午，村中老人手提篮子，内装饭菜、茶、米、糖、蜡烛到缅寺滴水。勐简大寨佤族在捂沙这一天的滴水仪式同汉族清明节扫墓是一样的，都是生者向死者表示祭奠和怀念。在当地还有这样一个不成文的规定：正常死亡者、死于村寨内部者，家人可以逢节日到缅寺中滴水，若是非正常死亡者、死于异地者，家人只能在缅寺外滴水，因为他们的灵魂无法进入缅寺。

第四，堆沙。这是节日期间仪式的最后一项，指到白沙水祈福。4月16日，是勐简大寨佤族一年一度泼水节中最隆重盛大的日子。这天清晨，村中老人要到缅寺献佛。早饭后，全村女子无论老少都穿上最传统的勐简大寨佤族服装，戴上最美的首饰，撑着色彩鲜艳的花伞，手持祈福"花"，向圣地白沙水前行。白沙水是一个地名，位于大寨村东3公里处，那里有一股清泉从白沙里渗出，泉水入口清凉甘甜，令人神清气爽，当地有"最美不过小姑娘，最好不过白沙水"的谚语，因而当地人将此地称为白沙水。那里除了白沙清泉，还有两棵根深叶茂的大青树，与老厂河的大青树分别屹立在大寨的东西两侧，成为保佑大寨的东西神树。到了白沙水后，佛爷和村中的长者用白线绕住青树，在树下点上两根蜡烛、放上一碗清水。准备完毕，佛爷开始念经祈福，经文大意为：

今天是一年一度的白沙水祈福日，我们穿戴整齐，手持祈福"花"献给你。请你将不吉利之物、引风沙雷电之物、带来疾病死亡之物、让百姓斗殴生气之物统统赶走，留下吉祥平安，留下顺利，留下祝福。保福保佑村寨兴旺，保福保佑人人身体健康，保福保佑六畜兴旺、五谷丰登。

佛爷边念经边向四周泼洒碗中的清水，意为驱逐不吉祥之物，将幸福平安留在树里，这样才能让神树永远保佑村寨和村民。佛爷念经结束后，盛装的人们手持"花"到白沙清泉、大花坛、大青树下插花祈福。祈福完毕，由佛寺中的小和尚带队返回缅寺。到达缅寺后，人们再次将祈福"花"插在堆沙台中，然后进入寺内点蜡烛祈福，祈求一年的快乐、平安、幸福。

通过这一系列的仪式，勐简大寨的泼水节才结束。

○ 穿黄衣的佤族

多彩中国节

泼水节

Chapter Three

Different Nationalities' Customs of the Water-Splashing Festival

The Water-Splashing Festival is the traditional festival of some minorities in Southwest China such as Dai, Bulang, De' ang and Achang. It spreads widely because of its rich contents. Water-Splashing Festival is the New Year in Dai calendar, so it is especially appreciated by Dai people. At the same time, the Water-Splashing Festival also covers almost every settlement of the nationalities that believe in the Southern Sect of Buddhism.

1. The Distribution of Water-Splashing Festival in China

According to the number and scale of participants, the Water-Splashing Festival mainly spreads over Xishuangbanna Dai Autonomous Prefecture, Dehong Dai and Jingpo Autonomous Prefecture, Menglian Dai, Lahu and Va Autonomous County, Gengma Dai and Va Autonomous County, Yuanjiang Hani, Yi and Dai Autonomous County, Xinping Yi and Dai Autonomous County and other areas in Yunnan Province.

Xishuangbana

Xishuangbanna Dai Autonomous Prefecture is the first-established ethnic autonomous prefecture in Yunnan Province, located in the southernmost part of the province. Xishuangbanna is the state-level ecological demonstration zone and the national scenic area, with colorful natural and cultural characteristics of "tropical rainforest, winter resort, harmonious homeland, mystical folk-custom", and is "a great place for Dai people in Southeast Asia to seek roots, for people in the North to escape the cold winter, and for tourists at home and abroad to be close to nature and pursue health." It is famous for its mystical natural landscape of tropical rainforest and ethnic customs, and is one of the hot tourist cities in China.

The Water-Splashing Festival held in Xishuangbanna every April 13 to 15 in the solar calendar enjoys great reputation, and is known as "Oriental carnival".

Tips for Tourism

Jinghong

Jinghong is the capital of Xishuangbanna Dai Autonomous Prefecture, located in the south of Yunnan Province and in the middle of Xishuang—banna Dai Autonomous Prefecture. Lancang—Mekong River, known as the "Oriental Danube", flows through the city, which is the main channel for China to enter Southeast Asia. This tourist border city has rich ethnic customs and charming subtropical scenery. There is the beautiful Peacock Lake in the city center, which reflects the upright oil palms, pattra trees, betel nut palms and coconut trees on both sides of the road.

Famous attractions:

Xishuangbanna Forest Park, Tropical Botanical Garden, Dai Garden, Wild Elephant Valley, Mengle Giant Buddhist Temple etc.

Best travel time:

From November to April, comfortable temperature, neither cold nor hot.

Dehong

Dehong Dai and Jingpo Autonomous Prefecture is located in China's southwestern border area. "Dehong" is the transliteration of Dai lauguage, "De" meaning below, "Hong" meaning Nujiang River, and "Dehong" meaning "the lower reaches of Nujiang River".

139

Joy in heart (Ruili, Yunnan Province)

Tips for Tourism

Ruili

Ruili is an important channel of Silk Road in the ancient south. It is also the transit point and distributing center of Sino−Burmese trade. Ruili is located in the southwest of Yunnan Province, and it is affiliated to Dehong Dai and Jingpo Autonomous Prefecture. It is 99km away by land from the capital city, Mangshi, and 890km from the provincial capi− tal, Kunming. It is the terminal point of No.320 State Road starting from Shanghai, and the intersection of Kunming−Ruili Road and Stilwell Road. Its northwest, southwest and southeast sides are linked with the mountains and villages of Burma. Now, it governs two zones: Jiegao Border Trade Zone and Wanding Economic Development Zone, three towns including Mengmao, Wanding and Nongdao, and three townships including Jiexi− ang, Huyu and Mengxiu.

Matters needing attention

The ultraviolet ray in Ruili is strong, so sunburn protection is neces—
sary outdoors. Please prepare sunshade umbrellas, and sunglasses, hats, and
sunblock. If coming to Ruili between July and September, you can wear
short—sleeved clothes, skirts, or a thin sweater.

Best travel time

The best travelling time to Ruili is from July to the mid of September.

Ruili is of a South Asia's tropical monsoon climate, including the
dry season and rainy season through the whole year, with the annual aver—
age temperature around 21 ℃. There is no snow here, nor cold winter,
but it is very hot in summer, with flowers blooming in all seasons.

Pu'er City

The city of Pu'er, with another name Simao, is a prefecture-
level city in Yunnan Province, located in the southwest of the
province. The spreading areas of the Water-Splashing Festival
in Pu'er are mainly Jinggu Dai and Yi Autonomous County
and Menglian Dai, Lahu and Va Autonomous County.

Tips for Tourism

Simao

Simao District, affiliated to Pu'er City, is situated in the south of
Yunnan Province, middle south of Pu'er, middle and lower reaches of
Lancang River. Simao District is the seat of the municipal party committee
and the government of Pu'er, the political, economic and cultural center
of Pu'er and also the transportation hub connecting southeast Asia. Simao
District is the starting point of the Ancient Tea—horse Road — the South—
ern Silk Route, and one of the three important customs cities in Yunnan
Province, ever known as the "land wharf of southeast Asia" and "silver
Simao".

Famous sights

The main ruins of Simao District include Shiping Guild Hall, Simao Confucian Temple, Simao Old Customs, the Ancient Tea—horse Road, the Observation Deck of Tea City, etc.

The Observation Deck of Tea City is constructed on the basis of the original ecological environment, not destroying the surrounding tea trees, with a little artificial carving and the observation deck put in the tea trees, and provides the public with a predominantly recreational place. On the Observation Deck, people can watch the undulating tea fields closely on the northwest side and overlook the beautiful Tea City of China; to the southwest, people can enjoy the natural ecological tea mountain, Ganhaizi Lake and scenic spot Meizi Lake Park, which is surrounded by mountains; far away are the endless pinus khasys. Enjoying the view here can make you feel relaxed and happy. Along the famous Ancient Tea—horse Road are winding mountains and crisscross gorges, with exquisite scenery, changeful climate and simple folklore customs. It is amazing that she had witnessed the rise and fall of pu'er tea trade, and is an important carrier of the profound pu'er tea culture.

Best travel time

All seasons are suitable.

Lincang and Yuxi

The spreading areas of the Water-Splashing Festival in Lincang City are mainly Gengma Dai and Va Autonomous County and Shuangjiang Lahu, Va, Bulang and Dai Autonomous County, while those in Yuxi City are Yuanjiang Hani, Yi and Dai Autonomous County and Xinping Yi and Dai Autonomous County.

Huayao Dais greeting at the village gate (Xinping, Yunnan Province)

Tips for Tourism

Huayao Dai

Huayao Dai is a name given to Dai people who reside in Xinping County and Yuanjiang County in the upper and middle reaches of the Red River. They are called so because their costumes are simple, elegant and gorgeous, especially the sash wrapping the waist layer upon layer, which is embroidered with gorgeous and exquisite patterns and dressed with flam—boyant tassels and silver bells. The name of Huayao Dai was first recorded in the Qing dynasty, with the Dai people living in the middle reaches of the Red River called "Huabaiyi". Huayao Dai is the name given to Dai nationality by other ethnic groups in the Republican period, which is composed of three branches: Daiya, Daisa and Daika. Dai people here not only are quite different in dress culture from Daile in South Yunnan and Daina in West Yunnan, but also have no faith in Buddhism, no writ—ten language, not celebrating the water—splashing festival, and retain the

143

original culture before Chinese Dai nationality's accepting the Buddhist culture impact of India.

Huayao Dai in Gasa and Shuitang of Xinping County call themselves Daisa, those in Yaojie of Xinping County and Ganzhuang of Yuanjiang County call themselves Daika, and those in Mosha of Xinping County and Dong'e Township of Yuanjiang County call themselves Daiya. The Huajie (flower street)Festival (also known as "the Ganhua Festival") is a grand festival for young men and women of Dai nationality to know each other, pay court to each other and choose their life partners. Huayao Dais' bamboo weaving, bamboo split headgears, waist baskets, silver jew—elry and potting have long enjoyed a good reputation.

Matters needing attention

When a Huayao Dai host is picking up food for the guest, the guest can not decline or shift it to someone else. Nor can the guest decline when the host serves wine, but it is ok to leave the rest in the wine cup. Huayao Dai people have the habit of chewing betel nuts, so most of their teeth are black. In fact, they regard this as beautiful to some extent.

Famous scenic spots

Xinping—Ailao Mountain Natural Reserve, Mopanshan National Forest Park, Xinhua Guzhou Wildwood, Yangwu Hotspring, etc.

Yuanjiang—Yuanjiang Ailao Terraced Fields, Colorful Gypsum Forest, Miaolian Temple, Nanuo Hani Cloud Sea Terraces, etc.

Best travel time

Summer and autumn are the best, especially around the sixth day of the fifth lunar month, when the grand Huajie (flower street) Festival of Huayao is celebrated.

Other regions

In addition to most of the autonomous prefectures and autonomous counties inhabited by Dai people holding large-scale Water-Splashing Festival activities, this festival is also an annual happy event for De'ang, Bulang and Achang nationalities. So it also has corresponding distribution and circulation in relevant areas that these nationalities inhabit.

De'ang people are mainly distributed in Mangshi, Ruili (including Wanding economic zone), Longchuan, Yingjiang, Lianghe of Dehong City, and there is also a small amount of distribution in Longyang District of Baoshan City, and Zhenkang, Gengma, Yongde County of Lincang City, and Lancang County of Simao City. Around Dehong section of the sino-burmese border line are De'ang settlements. The Water-Splashing Festival called "Flower-wateringFestival" by De'ang nationality is distributed in Ergucheng Village, Hexi Township, Lianghe County, Dehong Prefecture, Chudonggua Village and Bangwai Village, Santaishan Township, Mangshi City, Wuchalu Township and Mangshi Township of Mangshi City, Leimen Village of Ruili City, Zhenkang County of Lincang City and other places.

Bulang people celebrating the Water-Splashing Festival are mainly distributed in Menghai County, Jinghong City and Mengla County of Xishuangbanna, Simao District, Lancang Autonomous County and Jinggu Autonomous County of Pu'er City, Shuangjiang County, Gengma County, Zhenkang County and Yongde County of Lincang City. Among the county-level administrative regions above, Shuangjiang Lahu, Va, Bulang and Dai Autonomous County and Menghai County have the largest population of Bulang nationality and the most concentrated people who celebrate the Water-Splashing Festival. People in Shuangjiang County all celebrate this festival except those in Lingdi Village of Rubangbing Township who have no faith in Buddhism.Bulang people in the north of

Jinghong City and Kemu people of Bulang in Mengla County, Xishuangbanna do not celebrate this festival. Nearly all Bulang people in Lancang County and all Bulang people in Simao District and Jinggu County of Pu'er City celebrate this festival.

Achang is one of the eight localized minorities with a small population in Yunnan Province, which is mainly distributed in three nationality townships in Dehong Prefecture: Husa of Longchuan County, Nangsong and Jiubao of LiangheCounty,with the rest distributed in Mangshi, Longling County and Tengchong County of Baoshan City, and Yunlong County of Dali Prefecture. Achang is also a cross-border ethnic group; in Burma, it is known as "Maida" nationality, with a population of about 40,000, and mainly distributed in such places as Myitkyina of Kachin State and Kengtung of Shan State.

Now, in addition to the southwest ethnic nationality areas, with the population migration and culture spread, the Water-Splashing Festival with stronger performability will also be held each year between May and June in some tourist attractions such as Splendid China Folk Village, Shenzhen and Chinese Ethnic Culture Park, Beijing, attracting tourists to participate in and experience Dai culture.

While in Shishi City of Fujian Province, there is another kind of "the Water-Splashing Festival at Sea", which is the traditional folk custom festival of Han nationality of Fujian and Taiwan on both sides of Hanjiang, Shishi. The Dragon Boat Festival on the fifth day of the fifth lunar month, commonly known as "May Festival", is one of the oldest traditional festivals of Han nationality. The southern migration of the central Chinese people brought the Dragon Boat Festival custom in memory of Qu Yuan. According to the legend, after Qu Yuan jumped into the river, a lot of Chu people, being loath to see a virtuous official die, chased for the rescue by rowing boats. They fell over each other; but when chased to Dongting Lake, his body was invisible. This is the origin of the dragon boat race, and from then on, people will row dragon boats on May 5 each year for commemoration. On this day, the boats on both sides of Hanjiang will chase and splash water at sea, and in this joyous way, people wish for good luck, communicate friendship, and pray for peace and prosperity. Hence, the custom of "water-splashing at sea" came into being and was handed down from generation to generation for more than 300 years. It has become a kind of distinctive cultural custom crossing over Fujian and Taiwan, and is also the only custom of "the Water-Splashing Festival at Sea" in the world. The beautiful Xishuangbanna and the beautiful Hanjiang, different places, different minorities, have the same customs and the same emotion.

Jingpo girls during the festival (Longchuan, Yunnan Province)

2. The Water-Splashing Festivalof Dai Nationality

Dai nationality is one of the unique minorities in Yunnan Province. In a variety of illustrations, covers, film and television works, Dai girls wearing gorgeous tight skirts are always presented with watery flexibility and elegance. The movie *Peacock Princess* has long been synonymous with beauty and magic; the dancer Dao Meilan's *Water* and Yang Liping's *Peacock Princess* and *Spirit of the Peacock* take our breath away; the painter Yuan Xikun's *Water of Life* at Capital Airport has ever caused a big stir,and Ding Shaoguang's colorful paintings especially intensify the beauty of Dai women. In people's impression, the sight of Dai women will always remind people of what Jia Baoyu in *The Dream of Red Mansions* said,"Women are made of water." This should be the most appropriate comment for Dai women. Actually, with more knowledge of Dai nationality, people will find that not only Dai women are "made of water", even Dai men are also called "son of water", "Ludailunan" in Dai language. Dai nationality is "a nation of water"; they live by the water, like water, love water, and worship water; they have even created the unique water culture around the factor of "water", which constitutes the most important part of Dai culture. So someone ever said, "Dai nationality is like water: she can restrain herself, flowing through the valley and shallow creek, and also converging into vast water, rushing down vigorously; she is also good at reflecting her own color: when the sky is blue, she is blue; when the sky is red, she is red; she is, however, herself, pure and colorless." With the passage of time, in Dai people's heart, water is no longer a simple physical entity, but a mysterious strength infiltrating their life year after year. Dai nationality

148

and their ancestors living at the water countryside go together with water day by day. And the Water-Splashing Festival, which presents the closest relationship between Dai nationality and water, intensively implies Dai people's spirit meditation and thinking principle and reflects their concept of value and aesthetic taste that culture and art created for it has taken on unique national and local characteristics.

For Dai people, the Water-Splashing Festival, as their grandest festival, is actually their New Year, approximately between April 13 to April 15 in the solar calendar, and usually lasts 3 to 7 days. The Water-Splashing Festival, called "Sanghanbimai" in Dai dialect, is a traditional festival for Dai people to ring out the Old Year and ring in the New Year. The first day of the festival is the New Year's Eve, called "Wanduoshanghan" in Dai dialect, meaning ringing out the Old Year; the next day is called "Wannao", meaning an empty day, namely, this day is included neither in the Old Year nor in the New Year; the third day is New Year's day, which is called "Wanbawanma", namely "the day of the coming of King of Days". During the Water-Splashing Festival, Dai people in different villages are immersed in a jubilant atmosphere. On the first day of the festival, some riverside villages will hold dragon boat racing. Dai villages along Lancang River are especially lively, with tens of thousands of Dai people gathering from all directions to Lancang River to watch dragon boat race. On the empty day between New Year's Eve and New Year's day, Dai people in splendid costumes rush to different villages to attend large-scale *Ganbai* activities; young men and women cheerfully play the game of tossing embroidered parcels in the square, looking for their Mr./Miss Right. An "embroidered parcel" is commonly a square of 4 to 5 inches, sewn with various cloths of different colors, filled with cotton seeds, bombax ceiba seeds or chaff, four corners decorated with colorful cloths, with a cotton tape as the sling. As the sun sets, young women flock to the open field at the side of villages, only to find that young men have already been waiting there, standing in a row. Young women come over to be about 20 meters away from the young men, and throw flowers at them as a gift, which indicates the begining of the game of tossing embroidered parcels. At the other corner of *Ganbai* field, Gaosheng will be lit; with waves of people's cheering, Gaosheng bloom in the sky. In the evening, people will set off Kongming lanterns,which decorate the night sky colorfully. On New Year's day, people, without reference to age and sex, take a bath and put on clean clothes, and young men and women are even dressed up, wearing their most beautiful clothes and their favorite jewelry and flowers. Early in the morning, people carry the offerings to the Buddhist temple for

The elderly women of Dai nationality during the festival
(Yingjiang, Yunnan Province)

Danfo; every family will heap the sand into a sand tower of four to five feet high near the Buddhist temple, insert flowers and ticker tape, and listen to the Buddha chanting sutras beside the sand tower, and then hold the ceremony of washing the Buddha statue. After the ceremony, the carnival activity—splashing water, can not wait to start.

3. The Water-Splashing Festival of De'ang Nationality

De'ang people mainly inhabit Dehong Dai and Jingpo Autonomous Prefecture, Yunnan Province, and have a native language and mainly speak Dai language.

In April, while the snow in the northern part of China is just melting and the winter cold is not over yet, the land of peacocks—Dehong, is already full of flowers and spring is in the air. The Water-Splashing Festival of De'ang is quietly coming in the season with the chirping of birds and the fragrance of flowers. On the seventh day after the Tomb-sweeping Day every year, De'ang villages surrounded by trees and bamboo forests are all up. Dressed in a lattice tight skirt embroidered with colorful patterns and a straitjacket with silver buttons, De'ang girls shoulder the bamboo baskets loaded with bamboo buckets to celebrate the Water-Splashing Festival. The Water-Splashing Festival is originally a celebration activity for Dai New Year; De'ang people believe in the Southern Sect of Buddhism, so they also celebrate the coming of New Year in the form of the Water-Splashing Festival. The Water-Splashing Festivalof De'ang people is called the "Flower-watering Festival", and is now on the list of national intangible cultural heritage protection. But in the folk, this festival has not yet been established within De'ang people. Though on the whole, it is called the

Water-Splashing Festival or the Flower-watering Festival, the names in different branches are not the same: "Raomai" branch calls it "Bathing the Buddha Festival", "Bulie" branch calls it "Hongpula", "Liang" branch calls it "Shangjian", all of which mean bathing the Buddha. The Flower-watering Festival, which is called in De'ang language "Kuhubosangjian" or "kuhubo", means "watering flowers". "Sangjian" derives from the Indian Sanscrit, meaning "bathing the Buddha festival". Though the Flower-watering Festival is certified in the national intangible cultural heritage list, many De'ang people, especially those who inhabit mixed ethnics areas, still habitually call it the Water-Splashing Festival, or mix the Water-Splashing Festival with Flower-watering Festival, and still celebrate this festival in the traditional way.

De'ang costumes (Mangshi, Yunnan Province)

The Flower-watering Festival of De'ang is held in the middle of April in the solar calendar. Compared with the Water-Splashing Festival customs of Dai people, the Flower-watering

Festival of De'ang is not only "Bathing the Buddha Festival", but also "the festival of reminiscing and worshipping mothers". At the time, the younger generation of each family will prepare a basin of hot water, put it in the middle of the central room, call out their parents and other elders to sit there, kowtow and confess to them, and ask to forgive their unfilial behavior. The elders will also examine their yearly behavior where they have done a poor job of setting an example for the younger generation. Then, the younger generation will wash the elders' hands and feet, and wish each other to spend the next year in harmony and industry. If the parents have passed away, the elder brothers, elder sisters, elder sisters-in-law or elder brothers-in-law will become the objects of washing. About this peculiar custom of respecting the aged, there are mainly two legends spreading.

The first legend is a sad story. Long long ago, a De'ang widow raised her son to maturity very hard, pinch and scrape, until she became blind. When the son saw that his mother was not doing well as before, he was very dissatisfied and often scolded her. On the seventh day after a year's Tomb-sweeping Day, while the son was working uphill, he saw an unfledged young raven trying to find worms back and forth to feed an old and thin raven. The scene educated the son, who blamed himself for being inferior to the young raven "holding food in mouth to repay mother", and was determined to serve his mother well. Just then, the sick and hungry mother was groping the way to send meal to her son, but tumbled on half way. When she was awakened by the cool breeze, thinking that her son must be very hungry, she hurriedly struggled to climb uphill. While climbing, she heard her son running down from the hill. For fear of being scolded, she made up her mind to hit the big tree by the roadside, and died. The son came to apologize to his mother; seeing that his mother was frightened to death by him, he wept his heart out, but regretted in vain. When the son buried his mother, he cut down the tree and carved a statue of his mother to enshrine at home. From then on, on the seventh day after the Tomb-sweeping Day every year, the son would go uphill to collect Henry chestnut branches, and by dipping the clean water in the bamboo tube shouldered from the ravine, clean the statue immersed in warm water with petals, which later evolved into a custom. Since then, De'ang people celebrate the Water-Splashing Festival, during which they shoulder water with bamboo baskets, dip flower branches into water and splash each other, and wash hands and feet for the elderly.

The second legend stems from a more mysterious and ancient myth. In ancient times, the omnipotent epoch-making Lord Buddha, in order to help De'ang people handle the great events in production and life, came to the world from heaven with God's consent. In order not to arouse people's fuss, the Lord Buddha, after coming down to the earth, became a Buddha, living alone in the Buddhist temple. He did a lot of good things for the people, relieved many disasters, and was greatly respected and loved by the people. People would ask for his help for whatever difficulties. At first, people only went to him when they experienced joy, mourning, shelter, food and so on. Because he was the embodiment of wisdom, he had many ways to solve problems, and exactly to the right degree. Over time, various big or small businesses such as what kind of crop should be planted in which field, which young man should marry what kind of girl, which child should get what kind of name, which old man would live how long, would all come to him. Sometimes, when the husband and wife were not in peace, they would also seek for his conciliation, which made him restless day and night. He gradually felt that there were too many and too miscellaneous things in the world, but thinking of the industrious and kind De'ang people, he was reluctant to leave the world. The time permitted by God was up, and he was urged time and again to return to the heavenly palace. Although the Lord Buddha was still attached to De'ang people, he was afraid to be against God, and thus in worry he became seriously ill and was bedridden. People managed to find rare medicinal herbs far and near, and offered them to him. The Lord Buddha knew that God wanted to call his soul to the heavenly palace, so taking medicine would not help. One day, his condition suddenly deteriorated; all of the people came to ask him what he wanted. He only asked to carve a wooden statue in his appearance and took a bath for him. The people did so, and three days later, the outline of the statue was carved out. He opened his eyes, nodded, and said with satisfaction, "everything is all right", and then closed his eyes. After half a month, the Buddha's hands and feet were finished. The Buddha opened his eyes, said with a smile, "fair weather and good harvest," and closed his eyes again. After a month, the Buddha's eyes, ears, mouth and nose were all carved out. The Tomb-sweeping Day had passed then, and the Buddha, with his eyes wide open, looked over and over again at the statue, and said happily, "avoiding devils, human and animal disease-free". But people had no time to bathe him before he left the world. To show people's reminiscence and also complete his enjoining, people built on the spot an exquisite pavilion according to the style of Buddhist temple, placed the Buddha statue in the center of the pavilion, and did a big three-day *Ganbai*, and splashed water on the statue for three days. Since then, De'ang people have been splashing water every year, and gradually a festival has been formed, called "Sangen", meaning the Water-Splashing Festival.

The two legends have been handed down. With the continuous development of the society, De'ang people have attached new content to the Water-Splashing Festival. In the festival, people not only put on the festival costumes to, first of all, splash water on the Buddha or the Buddha statue,showing reminiscence and respect to ancestors and benefactors, but also scrub dust and offer birthday felicitations to the long-lived elders who are over sixty, to express their thanks and blessings. After these ceremonies, the young men and women will splash water on each other, especially on the newlyweds, wishing them a harmonious and happy life.

The Water-Splashing Festival of De'ang and that of Dai people are similar but different. Close to the festival, people are busy sewing new clothes, making rice cakes and making water-splashing tools like water dragons and buckets. Early on the first day of the festival, the believers bring various pre-prepared offerings from home to the Buddhist temple for Danfo. The offerings will be offered to the Buddha as soon as people enter the Buddhist temple. The Buddha will read to the believers a length of "Manggela" (blessing phrases), whose general content is, "Thank you for your food and materials, and I wish you ample food and clothing for generations, and wish your family good health, all the best, and a better next year than this year."

After the Danfo ceremony, the Buddha begins to invite the Lord Buddha, while the believers congregating in the Buddhist temple put their palms together, kneel on the floor devoutly, and listen to the Buddha's chanting:

The respectable Lord Buddha, we observe a festival today, and I come to ask for your instructions with all the households. We ask you to come out, and we will wash you up, hoping that you look better and that you consider our kindness. Please give us instructions as to our wrong doings in the past year, and hope for your forgiveness. In this year, we hope that the Lord Buddha will bless us more success, peace and happiness.

When the Buddha has finished this verse, the believers begin to chant in chorus under the guidance of the Buddha:

The respectable Lord Buddha, I believe in such Buddhism. At the same time, I demand myself not to steal, rob, beat, scold others, or do nasty things any longer. I will well believe it; only it will guide us to live a happy life, and make my heart walk on the road of integrity. After I believe in the Buddhism, I will respect the elderly, care for the children, and support our nation. We should heed what the Buddha says, what the elderly say, and do not take part in unpleasant activities such as fighting and brawling. We need to respect our parents, and love our nation. Parents educate us not to steal things, not to do bad things, not to rob other people's things, and even more not to make disgusting conduct. No matter what nations we meet, including those foreign nations, we are all friends and relatives, and should unite as one. Only in this way can we reside in harmony and acquire common development. These are traditionally handed down over generations, and let us believe so, which are worthy of respect.

The above chanting will last about half an hour. Then people take the Buddha statue from the Buddhist temple to the pavilion, and the dripping ritual starts: dripping clean water on the ground. And at the same time people recite the following text: "Various gods, we have worshipped you with water, and given you merits. Please help me remember my negligence and virtue, and at the same time bless that we would not go to the trouble, and would not make the same mistakes."

Then there will be girls who carry basins or buckets full of auspicious water to wash the dust from the Buddha statue. Before bathing the Buddha statue, the Buddha will lead the villagers to recite a text, whose general content is: "The respectable Lord Buddha, we have put you out, and in the following days we will wash you every day with fresh water, hoping you to be clean. Please bless us, we will be also clean." Through bathing the Buddha, people express sincerity to the Buddha with cleanliness, and also hope that the Buddha will give back cleanliness.

At this moment, the venerable elders will hold flowers, and after dipping water, gently splash to the surrounding crowd, blessing them and celebrating the beginning of the New Year. People begin to get excited and bless each other a happy New Year. Young people raise the bucket high above the head and splash water on the hands of the elderly, wishing them a happy, healthy and long life, while the elderly put out their hands, hold the water and read the greetings, congratulating and blessing the young people. At the end of the ceremony, people will take the elephant-foot drum as the leading, stand in a long line, flock to the spring or the riverside, singing, dancing, chasing each other and splashing water.

De'ang villagers filling "dragon groove" with water
(Mangshi, Yunnan Province)

The Water-Splashing Festival is not only the ceremony of De'ang people's celebrating the New Year, but also a good opportunity for young men and women to pay court to each other and find sweethearts. The custom of giving bamboo baskets as a present is popular among De'ang people. Before Tomb-sweeping Day, young men will sharpen their knives and cut down the best bamboos to make bamboo baskets. Three days before the Water-Splashing Festival, young men carefully weave the baskets well, and in the still of night, give the baskets respectively to all the girls participating in the dating activity. The most beautiful basket will be sent to his favorite girl, to express his love and test the girl's reaction. At the time, every girl can usually receive several bamboo baskets. But who does the girl really love? This is to see whose bamboo basket the girl will shoulder on the day of the festival. On the day, each girl will carry a delicate and beautiful bamboo basket on the back. But whose basket is this? This is a busy time for the young men, who open their eyes wide, gaze at the baskets on the girls, and carefully identify whether the bamboo basket his sweetheart carries is the one he gives her. As soon as the pairing lovers meet, they will splash water to each other and play to their hearts' content to express their excitement and joy. At this time, the bamboo basket is not only a token of love, but also an indispensable tool for the Water-Splashing Festival.

On the morning of the festival, young men, accompanying the girls carrying on the bamboo baskets, stand in a long line, and while beating the elephant-foot drums, they go to the well or ditch to carry clean water, and then come back to the temple on the edge of the stockaded village. The adult men then take out the largest mangs and the largest cymbals, and dance mang-cymbal dance with the accompaniment of the elephant-foot drums. While dancing, they lead all the people to go around the temple. After four or five laps, they stop dancing; gathering around the color dragon spraying water, the girls take turns to ascend the wooden support standing high above the color dragon, take out the bamboo tubes in the bamboo baskets slanting on one side of the body, and pour the clean water into the dragon. The color dragon will immediately spray water. And the cheering people dance with joy; the elephant-foot drum beats louder and louder; and the Water-Splashing Festival begins.

Unmarried men and women, some holding bamboo tubes, some carrying a vat, take from the inside of the bamboo tubes or the vat a bunch of light yellow Henry chestnut flowers, splash the water gently on each other's shoulder, blessing each other and greeting the coming of the New Year. The water-splashing will last three days. After the festival, each family will carry the clean water and raise the bamboo tubes, splash water on the elders' hands, wishing them a long life, and then wash their face and hands. Then they will carry water to other families, helping their elders wash face and hands, and treat the elders with water-splashing Baba. Until all the elders in the stockaded village have had water-splashing Baba, the Water-Splashing Festival will end in activities of respecting the old. It is important to note that the water-splashing method of De'ang people has a certain norm. For example, when splashing the elders, people can only use small bamboo tubes containing clean spring water, with flowers inserted, and let the water drip along the bouquet to elders' outstretched palms, while the water cannot be splashed on the body. When young men and women splash water on each other, they should also use bamboo tubes, and gently splash water down from the shoulder, while the head cannot be touched. When unmarried men and women splash water on the newlyweds, the impolite vulgarity is not allowed on both sides. Otherwise, the light punishment will be people's reprimand, while the severe punishment will be the deprival of the right to participate in the Water-Splashing Festival.

4. The Water-Splashing Festival of Achang Nationality

Achang, living in counties like Longchuan and Lianghe in Dehong Prefecture of Yunnan Province, is a nationality with just over 20,000 people, who exclusively inhabit Yunnan and belong to the cross-border ethnic minorities. Achang live together with other ethnic groups such as Dai, Jingpo, Lisu, and are greatly influenced by Dai nationality in all aspects of life and culture.

The Water-Splashing Festival of Achang is divided into

161

several processes such as picking flowers uphill, Danfo, giving offerings to the Buddha, bathing the Buddha and blessing each other by splashing water. The seventh day after the Tomb-sweeping Day is the beginning of Achang Water-Splashing Festival. On the morning of the day, people, without reference to age and sex, put on their holiday costumes and gather fresh flowers, which are inserted by women on the head and pinned by men on the chest. Around 4 pm, all the middle-aged and young men of the stockaded village gather in front of the Buddhist temple. Two dragon-phoenix flags lead the way; a person in the front is wielding a Husa knife, while several people behind are dancing the elephant-foot drum dance; people go forward to the mountain with great strength and vigour, firing all the way. After climbing up the mountain, people play the firecrackers and kowtow in front of the Henry chestnut tree, and then pick the Henry chestnut flowers and azaleas. After that, everyone becomes cheerful, waving the flower branches and indulging in singing and dancing. After dancing enough folk dances of Achang, people return to the stockaded village beating the elephant-foot drum all the way. Women in the village have already prepared Perilla Baba; as soon as they hear the flower-picking team informing by firing powder shotgun, they immediately choose a dozen of girls to greet outside of the village holding Perilla Baba. The men who have picked flowers present flowers to the girls, while the girls send basins of Perilla Baba to the flower pickers, then they sing and dance together, and go back to the village. The elderly have set up bamboo poles in front of the Buddhist temple. People bundle the flowers round and round the poles to make a flower tower. Some villages make it into a bamboo sedan, and call it "bridal sedan" with flowers stuck in. It is about 10 at night, people not only feel reluctant to disperse, but also they sing and dance around the flower tower and bridal sedan deep into the night.

On the second and the third day, people start to "pour the flower water". Men beat the elephant-foot drums, mangs and cymbals, open a way carrying flags of four colors in front, while the girls stand in a long row behind; they shoulder clean water from the river to splash the flower tower and bridal sedan, and pour the water into the bamboo dragon to spray the Buddha worshipped in the bridal sedan.

On the fourth night, the young men meet together to visit another village. As soon as they enter the village, the girls gathering together invite them to sleep in a girl's home, while the girls go to another girl's home, kill chickens according to the number of the young men, then make eight dishes in the way of frying, stir frying, boiling and stewing, to arouse the young men's affection with their superb cooking. At 2:00 in the morning, after placing on the round table a bowl of a chicken head, a bowl full of rice wine and a pair of chopsticks, one set for each young man, the girls go to invite the young men to dine: "Young men, we have cooked some food, please go to have a taste." The young men intended to "drop around", but they were asked to sleep upon arrival, how would they go to sleep? They lie in bed with eyes and ears open, waiting for the good news. Hearing the girls' voice, they are afraid to behave boldly, so they pretend to be too shy to open their mouth. The girls see no response, so they invite again, then the young men say in chorus, "Let's go to eat cheekily." They get up and follow the girls. After being seated at the table, they say some courtesy to each other, and sing in antiphonal style until dawn.

After such a contact, lovers form a close relationship, and songs become more touching. The young men will return to their village, and before leaving, they will hide the chicken money pooled beforehand in the wall chinks or under the bowls, and leave it for the girls to find. Then, each man takes the chicken head in his bowl and says goodbye to the girls. They have already planted the seeds of love through this activity.

Achang "Dengwoluo" dance during the Water-Splashing Festival
(Lianghe, Yunnan Province)

Tips for Tourism

Husa Township of Achang Nationality

Husa Township is one of the only three ethnic townships of Achang nationality in China, located in the northwest of Longchuan County, De-hong Prefecture. The government resident of Husa Township, Jiexiang Village, is 53 km from that of Longchuan County, Zhangfeng Town. There are multi-ethnic groups living in Husa, with the majority of Achang.

Main attractions

The most famous in Husa is the forging craft of Achang Husa knife, which has been included in the list of the national intangible cultural heritage protection. The forging craft of Husa knife is mainly concentrated in six villages: Panle, Huzao, Longguang, Xiangjie, Mingshe and Mangbing.

Best travel time

All seasons are suitable.

5. The Water-Splashing Festival of Bulang Nationality

The Water-Splashing Festival is also a traditional festival of Bulang, which is popular in the inhabited area of Bulang in Xishuangbanna. Bulang nationality is only endemic to Yunnan all over the country, and is an cross-border ethnic minority. They mainly reside in Bulang Mountain and mountain areas of Xiding, Bada and Daluo, Menghai County, Xishuangbanna, and the rest are scattered in places like Lincang and Pu'er. The former Bulangs called themselves different names because they lived in different areas. After the foundation of the People's Republic of China, they are collectively named Bulang nationality according to the ethnic will.

The inhabited areas of Bulang are mostly in the subtropical mountains, which are between 1,500 and 2,300 meters above sea level. The lofty and steep mountains are densely covered with the towering and shading primeval forests. The rainfall here is abundant, frost-free in four seasons, and rich in tung oil, Cinnamomum camphora and other trees of economic value. The Bulangs are mainly engaged in agriculture, growing dry rice, cotton and tea, and their habitation is one of the world famous producing areas of Pu'er tea.

The "Water-Splashing Festival" of Bulang nationality has many titles, including "Sangkan festival", "Songkan festival",

"Sangkan Bimai festival" , "Sangkan festival"and so on. It is a grand New Year festival of Bulang, which is held on the 7th day after the Tomb-sweeping Day in lunar March, namely from the 13th April to 15th April of the solar calendar. Despite the different titles, they all originated from the transliterated words of the the Southern Sect of Buddhism, roughly including the meaning of "worshipping the Sun-god", "welcoming the new harvest"and "Danfo". The main activity during the festival is to splash water on each other to greet the Sun. The day before the Water-Splashing Festival every year, young men and women of the stockaded villages take bamboo boxes and bamboo baskets to dredge the sand in the river, carry back to the Burmese temple, and pile up the sand and worship the Buddha in front of the temple. Before sunrise the next day, people will be neatly dressed, with Henry chestnut flowers and Chinese toon branches in hand, and rally at the end of the village. While beating drums, young men head for the Burmese temple in line, and insert flowers and tree branches in the sandpile, which will be repeated three to five times every day. In the east of the village, people will also put up a chuppah, set up an altar table, on which are such things like glutinous rice, wine, meat and bananas, and see moonset off and greet the sunrise under the host of the headman. Facing the rising sun spurting out in the east, people are singing and dancing joyously, thanking the sun for giving the world warmth and vitality. After the breakfast, people go in droves to the Buddhist temple to celebrate the arrival of a new day by inserting flowers, bathing the Buddha, giving blessings by splashing water,and piling up sand towers, playing bamboo balls, singing and dancing, and playing the game of tossing embroidered parcels. At night, young men and women will sing and dance to their hearts' content, which is really a bustling scene. Now, compared with the past, the contents of the festival have changed a lot; in addition to the previous traditional activities, there are also recreational programs and sports competition, which make it more welcome by people.

Bulangs dancing "Bee bucket drum dance" at the village during the Water-Splashing Festival (Shuangjiang, Yunnan Province)

Tips for Tourism

The Hometown of Pu'er Tea: Menghai

Menghai County is located in the southwest of Yunnan Province and the west of Xishuangbanna Prefecture, adjacent to Jinghong City in the east, Pu'er City in the northeast, Lancang County in the northwest, and Burma in the west and south. Menghai is not only one of the regions with the largest population of Bulang nationality in China, but also the home—

town of "pu'er tea" and the first place of tea production in China. There are many tea gardens here, including the wild "King of Tea of 1700–year history and over–800–year tea trees of artificial cultivation. Menghai County has rich ethnic customs, and the "Water–Splashing Festival" of Dais, "Gatangpa Festival" (Gatangpa in Hani language means recovery or resurrection) of Hanis, "Tower–enlarging Festival" of Lahus and "Sangkan Festival" of Bulangs all display the unique local folk customs and culture.

Main attractions

The main scenic spots include the Jingzhen Octagon Pavilion, the One–tree Forest, Daluo Forest Park, Manduanfo Temple, King of Wild Tea Trees in Bada, Manluanhui Mosque, and Mengbang Reservoir.

Best travel time

All seasons are suitable.

6. The Water-Splashing Festival of Va Nationality

The Vanationality mainly inhabit the southern part of the Nushan Mountains located in the west of the Lancang River and the east of the Salween River. It is one of the oldest ethnic minorities in Southwest Yunnan, endemic only to Yunnan Province in China, and is a cross-border ethnic minority. The Va nationality has a long history and rich culture. Because of its numerous branches, the customs vary. And most of its traditional festivals are related to folk religion. But there are also some Va people who believe in the Southern Sect of Buddhism, influenced in culture by Dai nationality, incorporating the Water-Splashing Festival into the festival system of their ethnic subline. The Va nationality of Dazhai Village, Mengjian Township, Gengma Dai and Va Autonomous County is a typical case. The Va people here belong to Yerong lineage of Ale Va branch, and for their earthy yellow clothes, they are also called "yellow-clothes Ava". The festival culture of the Va nationality of Dazhai Village is rich and colorful, but is different from Va festivals of other habitats. Among the numerous festivals, the Water-Splashing Festival is one of the most solemn and most distinctive festivals, which most intensively embodies the traditional culture of Dazhai Village.

The Water-Splashing Festival of Dazhai Village, also called "Sand-piling Festival", is the most solemn and grandest festival of Dazhai over the year. In addition to water, "sand" as the carrier presents the difference in customs of the Water-Splashing Festival from other nationalities, which intensively displays local characteristics of the Water-Splashing Festival. The Water-Splashing Festival of Va nationality begins four days after the Tomb-sweeping Day every year and lasts eight days. At the time, the dry season will be over, the rainy season is approaching, so it is also a festival seeing off the old and welcoming the new. The festival originated from a legend:

Once upon a time, there lived a man who sinned. Feeling guilty, he fetched clean silver sand from rivers in deep mountains every day, confessed to the Lord Buddha while spraying the sand around the Burmese temple, praying for the Lord Buddha's mercy. Touched by his sincerity, the Lord Buddha absolved his sins and let him make a fresh start. After that, people will take the sand to pile up in the Burmese temple, whether they have sins or not, in order to eliminate their sins or pray for the Lord Buddha's blessings to go smoothly in the upcoming year. For a long time, delivering sand, taking sand, covering sand and piling sand have become the four main themes of the festival that remain alive today.

The Water-Splashing Festival of Dazhai Village is made up

of a series of rituals around the topic, the sand.

First, delivering sand. The so-called delivering sand is that the villagers deliver the clean sand taken from the rivers in deep mountains during the year to the Burmese temple. According to the Va people of Dazhai, the sand is the most immaculate fetish which can ward off evil spirits, and spraying sand and worshipping the Buddha can bring the blessings of the Buddha. This belief makes delivering sand the longest-running activity in the Water-Splashing Festival of Dazhai Va nationality, which lasts from April 9 to April 13. During these five days, the activity of delivering sand goes incessantly. Every morning, the little monks in the Buddhist temple will lead the young men in the stockade to beat the drums and knock on mangs, and take turns to converge at the village center to form a sand-delivering procession. Hearing the sound of mangs or drums, the villagers will put on their traditional clothes, take the clean sand fetched from rivers in deep mountains through the year to converge in the square, and then deliver the sand to the sand-piling stage in the Burmese temple under the little monks' lead. While spraying sand, they pray, "Please bless us, smooth going, no diseases, no disasters, good harvest and flourishing breeding". When this is over, people go into the Burmese temple one by one, lighting candles, kowtowing and praying for blessings from the Lord Buddha.

Second, taking sand. It is to take clean sand from rivers in deep mountains and deliver it to the Burmese temple. Early this morning, led by the little monks of the Buddhist temple and following the team beating drums and knocking on mangs, the villagers head to Laochang River, which is about 9 kilometers away from the west of Dazhai, to take sand. Laochang River is far from the village, and the road to there is rough and rugged. The water there is crystal clear, and two big banyan trees of a thousand years are standing there majestically.The Va nationality of Dazhai see the banyan tree as "Sacred Tree", and the worship to it is very pious.so during the yearly Water-Splashing Festival, the sacrifice to banyan trees in Laochang River is an essential activity. When the villagers reach Laochang River, they first take a bath there, then go up to the upper reaches and take clean sand where almost no one enters during the ordinary days. After taking sand, people dance around banyan trees for entertainment. The monks of the Buddhist temple light two candles under banyan trees and pray for blessings. With the blessings, the villagers insert the blessing "flowers" around banyan trees, which means the end of sacrifice to banyan trees of Laochang River. Then people dance all the way back to the Burmese temple. Back to the village, the young people and children in the village carry water containers in hand, splash water towards those who have returned after taking sand, thanking them for taking sand in Laochang River after an arduous journey to pray for the whole village, and also wishing the other side good luck and peace. Upon arrival at the Burmese temple, they scatter the clean sand taken from Laochang River to the surrounding sand-piling stages while praying. When the sand-piling ceremony is finished, people go into the Burmese temple one by one, light candles and kowtow to the Lord Buddha. Only in this way could all the wishes be known to the Lord Buddha and blessings of the Lord Buddha be acquired.

Third, covering sand. This refers to stopping all activities related to the sand and washing the Buddha statue. On the early morning of April 15, some men in the village hold gourds in hand to collect water from the mountain, while some other men set up a scaffold for washing the Buddha statue in front of the Burmese temple. They lift the Buddha statue out and put it on the scaffold. There are four sinks around the scaffold aiming at the statue; after fetching water from the mountain, men climb up the tower and slowly pour the water into the sinks, and water flows down from the sinks and onto the Buddha statue, and feeds into the water catcher under the Buddha statue. At this time, the villagers will wash their faces with the water in the water catcher. They believe that the water can wash away sickness and bring health and beauty. After that, people splash water on the surrounding companions, blessing them with good health and smooth going. After all the water is used up, the Buddha directs people to carry the Buddha statue back to the temple, pull down the scaffold, and wait for the old villagers to come and drip water. In the afternoon, holding baskets filled with food, tea, rice, sugar and candles, the old villagers go to the Burmese temple to drip water. The dripping-water ceremony of Va nationality of Dazhai on the day of covering sand is the same as the tomb sweeping of Han nationality on Tomb-sweeping Day, both of which express the commemoration and remembrance of the living to the dead. There is such an unwritten rule locally: for those who died normallly or died in the village, their family can go to the Burmese temple on holidays to drip water; for those who died abnormally or died in foreign places, their family can only drip water outside of the Burmese temple, because their soul cannot enter the Burmese temple.

Fourth, piling sand. This is the last step of the festival

ceremony, refering to praying for blessings in White-sand Water. April 16 is the most solemn day of the annual Water-Splashing Festival for the Va nationality of Dazhai Village. Early this morning, the elderly in the village will go to the Burmese temple and give offerings to the Buddha. After breakfast, all the village women, regardless of their age, will put on the most traditional clothes of the Va nationality of Dazhai and the most beautiful jewelry, carry colorful umbrellas, hold praying "flowers", and go towards the holy land White-sand Water. White-sand Water is the name of a place, which is located 3 kilometers from the east of Dazhai Village. There is a clear spring effusing from the white sands; the spring water tastes cool and sweet, which is quite refreshing. So there is such a local proverb, "The most beautiful is the little girl, while the best is white-sand water", and so the local people call the place White-sand Water. Apart from the white-sand Spring, two lush banyan trees are also standing here; together with the banyan trees in Laochang River, they respectively guard the east and west side of Dazhai, and become the sacred trees that bless Dazhai. When reaching White-sand Water, the Buddha and the elders of the village circle banyan trees with white thread first, and light two candles and put a bowl of clean water under the trees. When everything is ready, the Buddha begins to chant sutras for blessings. The scripture briefly means:

Today is the annual blessing day of White-sand Water. We are neatly dressed, and offer "flowers" to you. Please drive away the ominous thing, those that can bring thunderstorm, lightning, diseases and death, and those that can make people fight and angry. And leave over auspiciousness and peace, smooth going, and blessings. Bless villages with prosperity, bless everyone with good health, and bless domestic animals with thriving and grains with good harvest.

While chanting, the Buddha splashes the clean water in the bowl around, meaning to drive away the unlucky things and leave over peace and happiness in the trees, and only in this way can the scared trees always bless the villages and villagers. After the Buddha's prayer is over, the well-dressed people, with "flowers" in hand, go to insert flowers and pray for blessings at the White-sand Spring and the big flowerbeds, and under the banyan trees. At the end of the prayer, they return to the Burmese temple under the lead of the little monks in the Buddhist temple. After arriving at the temple, people once again put the blessing "flowers" in the sand-piling stage, and then enter the temple to light candles and pray, praying for a year of peace and happiness.

Through the series of ceremonies, the Water-Splashing Festival of Dazhai will be over.

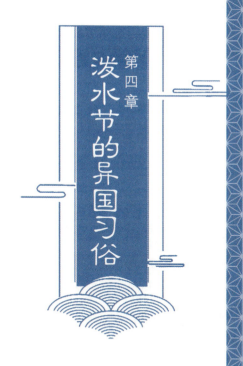

第四章

泼水节的异国习俗

泼水节源于印度，后为佛教所吸收，成为东南亚和南亚泰国、缅甸、老挝和印度的传统节日。但在不同国家，泼水节中呈现的习俗差异较大。

来到泰国亲身参加泼水节，人们的感受会很不一般。泼水节在泰国叫"宋干节"，是泰国民间最隆重的传统节日。每年 4 月 13 日至 15 日连续举行 3 天，内容十分丰富，包括僧侣行善、洒水沐佛、敬拜长辈、花车游行、歌舞、放生等，但人们能见到的最大众化的形式就是"全民打水仗"。

泼水节活动最盛的地方是泰国北部清迈府及周围的府县。节日前夕，街上挂满了泰国国旗，插满了各色的经幡，沿街各处搭好了台子。人们纷纷准备好水瓶、水瓢、水枪、水桶等泼水器具一应俱全。4 月 13 日一到，整个清迈一夜之间变成了一座水城。主战场设在城中央四周的街道上。因为这里有护城河，取水非常方便，可以随时补充水源，加上又是城中心，行人较多，热闹异常。凡有行人、摩托车、汽车经过，守候在街旁的人们便将水泼去。行人不用走多远，便被水浇透了。路过的摩托车和汽车也纷纷被"冲凉"，坐在摩托车上的人自不用说，一个个都成了"落汤鸡"。开车的人先有防备，就关住车窗，但一桶桶水仍从天而降。驾驶窗前全是水花，完全遮住了驾驶员的视线，车在"水阵"中突围。如果一时忘了关窗，那么

176

车里很快会变成一片汪洋。除了人和人大战、人和车大战外，更精彩的是车和车大战。泼水的勇士们坐在事先准备好的"战车"（一种敞篷的小货车）上，满街相互寻衅，乘双方错车的机会，将一瓢瓢、一盆盆、一桶桶水疯狂地泼向对方。整个清迈城里，到处水花飞溅，平地三尺水。笑声、叫声、歌声、欢呼声、汽车的高音喇叭声交织成一片，处处都变成了欢乐的海洋。

仔细观察，这里人们泼水的方式还各有不同。有斯文泼水的，仅仅只是用水瓶轻轻向行人身上泼洒；有"野蛮"泼水的，准备好一大盆水，使尽力气向人们身上倾倒；还有温柔泼水的，那是护城河边或公园里的恋人泼水。一对对情侣置狂热的泼水人群于不顾，找一个相对偏僻的角落，互相拥抱着，各拿一个瓶子向对方头上轻轻浇水。水从头顶一直流下，湿透了全身，也暖遍了全身。除了泼水祝福外，人们还要互抹香粉。节日这几天，天天从清早就有人守候在街边自己的"阵地"上，并各自准备好了各种水具和香粉。只要有人从那里经过，就一哄而上泼水和用香粉抹脸。被泼的人不仅全身湿透，脸上也成了"花脸"，但谁也不介意，因为这是幸福和吉祥的象征。

有趣的是，节日中街上骑摩托车的小姑娘似乎格外多，而且多是"义无反顾"地冲向"水阵"，惹得泼水的小伙子格外兴奋和卖力。他们纷纷把骑摩托车的姑娘拦下，又是"浇"水，又是抹粉。刚见到这种情形，初来者还会抱怨这些小伙子是否做得过分。等看到被泼被抹的姑娘不仅不生气，反而还笑逐颜开，继续去"自投罗网"，才发现这是愿打愿挨、两相情愿的事。真是有趣之至。

当然，如果是碰到外国游人，泼水者一般很客气，会征求意见后再给他们泼水或抹香粉。有的外国人人还加入到泼水的人群，也事先准备了泼水的工具，闹得比当地人还欢。多数外国人并不参加泼水，而是站在旁边看热闹。据说曾有一个外国人不知道此地的风俗，

177

泼水节那天从街上过被人"意外"地泼了一身，非常生气，就投诉到有关部门，控告当地人"骚扰"他。结果人家不受理，理由很简单：这是泰国最盛大的节日，当地人的行为不是骚扰，而是友好。

○泰国全民泼水节盛况（泰国清迈）

泼水节是泰国举国欢庆的狂欢节。节日期间，不仅是在城市，就是在远离城市的乡村小镇、偏远农村，人们也被调动起来投入到狂欢之中。在从清迈往古都素可泰的公路两边，可以看到沿路都有以年轻人为主的泼水大军，守住自己设在路边的"阵地"。他们顶着火辣的太阳，冒着40多度的高温，守望着过路的人和车。由于过路的人和车不多，加上过往的汽车又多关着车窗、开得又快，他们寻找泼水的"目标"并没有那么容易。参与过该地区泼水节的人总会对公路边那些皮肤黝黑、拿着水桶和水枪、忍受着烈日暴晒的泰国小孩印象深刻，他们欣喜而又兴奋地一心等着有人或车路过而把水泼过去。

○节前装饰一新的泰国佛寺（泰国曼谷）

二

缅甸泼水节

相比泰国，缅甸的泼水节习俗更为传统和丰富。每年公历 4 月 13 ~ 16 日是缅甸人民迎接缅历新年的传统节日——泼水节，这是缅甸人一年中最隆重、最热闹的时刻。

关于缅甸泼水节的来历，传说不一。普遍的一种说法是：有一年，缅王在宫中遇到神仙下凡，龙心大悦，命人用香料和清水混合，泼洒在文武百官的身上，表示涤旧除污，迎新接福。根据缅甸的传统信仰，人生在世，多多少少都是有罪的。人们相信可以用干净的水来洗刷这些罪过，净化心灵与思想，从而在新年来临之际确保自己是清白之身。缅甸人大多信奉佛教，男女老少举止斯文，谦逊有礼，可到了泼水节，他们就尽情宣泄，无所顾忌。年轻人可以从早到晚恣意狂饮，醉酒当歌。

缅历一年有 12 个月，每个月不仅各有名称，而且还有独特的含义，每个月都有一个传统节日。缅甸的第一个月被称为"达固"，意思是换岁之月、新年开始之月，泼水节就在这个月举行。泼水节是缅甸全民性的盛大传统节日，在缅语中称为"丁键"。"丁键"这个词来源于梵文，是"过渡、变更或转移"的意思，也就是从旧的一年转换到新的一年。泼水节是缅历旧年之末，所以缅甸新年是在泼水节的最后一天举行。人们为了把旧年的污秽洗去，迎接新的一年，就在这个转换的时期互相泼水。泼水节期间，正是缅甸一年之中最炎热的时期，泼水象征着温馨、清凉和吉祥。

按月份算，缅历和公历前后相差 3 个多月，缅历一月初一为公历 4 月 16 或 17 日。缅甸泼水节通常在公历 4 月 13 日至 16 日。缅甸人都相信泼水节是帝释天神降临人间考察人类善恶的日子，所以第一天是迎接日，第二天是降临日，第三天是巡察日，第四天是起驾回天日。因而泼水节一般要进行 4 天。节日期间，人们呈现出众多的当地民俗。

泼水

在缅甸，4 月份是一年之中最炎热的季节。大家互相泼水过年，既可以感受到节日带来的喜悦，又可以炎热的夏日带来难得的清凉。泼水节时的水被缅甸人认为是吉祥和幸福的象征，洒在身上能使身体健康。缅甸民间有一个说法，如果在泼水节期间没有被他人泼水，没有淋到泼水节的圣水的话，就会经常生病，而在泼水节期间被节日的圣水淋湿是不会生病的。但在泼水节期间，有三种人不会被水泼身，一是穿着袈裟的僧侣，二是老年人，三是孕妇。缅甸人泼水有两种泼法，分为文雅型与狂野型。所谓文雅型，也就是传统的泼法，用香樱桃花枝，从银钵中蘸取浸有檀香或香水的清水，轻轻地向别人身上抖洒。现在这样的泼法已经很少见了，只有对一些领导人或贵宾进行。至于狂野型，主要是青年之间对泼。现代的缅甸泼水节包含了人们步行或者乘车穿越在大马路上让别人泼。人们喜欢整桶整盆地泼，有的人甚至用水龙管喷射。泼的水往往是由大冰块溶化的冰水，泼在身上，让人冰冻到骨头里去，被泼的人也不会生气，人们被泼得愈多，就愈高兴。除此之外，不分男女、不分职业、不论身份，彼此之间，就算是素不相识，也可以相互泼水。如今大城市里许多人都喜欢乘着敞篷泼水车到泼水站去参加泼水节。

一旦进了4月份，缅甸每个城市的主要街道两旁一下子会出现许许多多的临时舞台，也叫做泼水站，是由市民、企业自发组织或由政府出面搭建而成。有的宏大气派，有的小巧玲珑，但共同的作用就是向过往的行人和车辆尽情泼水。泼水站周围，到处可见年轻人狂欢的场面：舞台中央男女青年载歌载舞，他们手持各式各样的塑料水枪，手舞足蹈，如痴如醉，尽情地宣泄，无所顾忌。在泼水站露天舞台上，身着节日盛装的缅甸少女在欢快地跳着传统的舞蹈。舞台上的其他年轻人手拿水管向台下观看者喷水。舞台临街一边，有些人手执水管把水洒向过往的人群和车辆。一辆辆敞篷泼水车从泼水平台前依次缓缓通过，车上的人们更愿意在台下多逗留一会，甘心接受这清凉的祝福。人们被泼得越多越高兴，因为水象征着幸福。现代的缅甸泼水节已经被狂野的泼法完全取代了。

跳舞

在缅甸，泼水节前两个月就到处是泼水节歌声，不论大城市还是小乡村都能听到家家户户发出的欢乐歌声。人们不仅能听到曼德勒谬玛乐团最有名的传统泼水节歌曲《都波都波》《瓦城花朵》《泼水节的雨》《庇荫于曼德勒山》等优美的歌声，欢乐的其他现代舞曲也覆盖了整个泼水节时期。节日期间，无论城乡，到处可以看到在临时搭起的彩棚上，美丽的姑娘们在跳缅甸传统泼水节舞。露天舞台有各式各样的演出，有优美的集体歌舞，也有时髦的现代舞。

○缅甸欢庆泼水节（缅甸仰光）

布施食品

在新年的第一天，缅甸人喜欢做各种各样的小吃。在各个地方举行捐赠食品这个活动叫做"Studitha"，源于梵文，是"四面八方"的意思，意为欢迎来自四面八方的每一个人参与。组织者会给每个参与者提供免费的食物（通常是传统小吃）。最有代表性的小吃是"泼水节汤圆"，有时候青年们为了嬉闹，会在汤圆里放入辣椒、硬币等物。吃到有硬币的汤圆表示有运气，即使有人吃到了辣椒也不会生气，大家嘻嘻哈哈的就过去了。著名的传统食品还有"籤鱼儿"，这是一种用石花胶、琼脂、糖水等制成的冷饮食品，用米粉做成短条状，吃的时候浇上椰子肉汁和红糖水或白糖水。也有些人在自己家做大量的小吃，请亲戚朋友来家做客，或者给邻居或亲戚家送过去，这样在新年之际，布施食物成了缅甸的传统习俗。

送新年花

4月的缅甸，沉浸在一片水、花交融的世界。在泼水节期间，有一种叫做"紫檀花"的花恰好开放。紫檀花是缅甸的国花，娇小，呈淡黄色，不算艳丽，但是此花一年仅开一次，一次只有一天按时盛开，所以缅甸人们很珍惜这个一年只开一次的圣花。新年快来临的时候，总要下一场雨。一般在4月以前的3～4个月左右不下雨，但一到新年时却突然下起雨来。这第一场雨叫新年雨。下了一场新年雨过后，整个缅甸的紫檀花都开了，这种被缅甸人民尊敬的花给全国各地带来了动感与活力，并以它特有的芳香，给缅甸人民送来新年的祝福和希望。紫檀花朵绽开以后，每个缅甸妇女的头上都会插上花朵。抬眼望去，到处是一片黄色，所以透过花朵就能感受到泼水节的气息。紫檀花可以说是缅甸泼水节的标记。紫檀花还是男女青年们的爱情信物，因为它一年只开一次，人们用它来比喻对爱情的忠诚和信义。小伙子会将自己从树上摘取的紫檀花给自己喜欢的姑娘，如果姑娘接受了并插在头上，就表示接受了小伙子的追求。

○缅甸泼水节中的少女（缅甸仰光）

守戒

　　泼水节是缅甸传统节日中最被人们重视的节日。此时此刻，不仅仅是人们娱乐的时期，也是积功德和善行的好时期。泼水节期间，缅甸有换年视察之说，这个说法是佛教进入缅甸后才演变过来的传说，也是佛教与缅甸民俗融合而演变的传说。据说，玉皇大帝为了视察人们一年内的善恶因果，派出使者去往人间。使者在除夕那一天从天而降来视察民间。他一手持金贝叶，一手持狗皮书。善者记录在金贝叶上，恶者记载在狗皮书上。所以缅人喜欢在泼水节期间守五戒、八戒，到寺庙、佛塔拜佛颂经。缅甸人虔诚信仰佛教，守五戒是每天必须做的事情，戒律为不杀生、不偷盗、不说谎、不冒犯别人妻女、不喝酒。泼水节期间，人们通常到寺庙守八戒。守八戒是在五戒的基础上，增加了不坐不睡高大华丽的床、不打扮；不听歌跳舞；中午12点过后到第二天凌晨5点，不吃食物，只能喝水等三戒。通常都是老年人到寺庙里守戒、听佛爷讲佛经、修道、修行等。也有一些人会带自己的儿女或孙辈一起到寺庙行善。

浴佛

浴佛在泼水节第一天举行。人们在自家的佛堂中供奉鲜花、香和蜡烛，然后用清水来"浴佛"，为佛像洗尘。目的是求佛祖保佑全家身心健康，岁岁平安。也有人去庙里参加浴佛活动。

放生

历时 4 天的泼水节后，便开始缅历新年。新年的第一天清晨，政府通常在公园举行放生仪式，象征性地将牛和羊放生。普通老百姓也自己买来将要被杀的活鱼放生到河里，或者是寺庙中的鱼塘。为了行善积德，放生成为缅甸人民新年的习俗之一；不仅可以放生鱼，也可以放活鸟。

出家仪式

家长喜欢在泼水节期间送自己的儿子去寺庙当小沙弥，以表示对佛的真诚奉献。出家是缅甸人一生中最大的事情，男孩只有出家后才算成人。将孩子送往寺庙是一件很荣耀的事情。在缅甸，男孩入寺的静修生活，时间可长可短，最短为一星期就可以还俗，今后要静修还可以再出家，次数不限，也有的是终身当和尚。更长的则是几个月、几年。缅甸的男孩子都喜欢在泼水节期间出家，从迎接日到新年一般出家 5 天。人们特别在新年时为了吉祥而出家，目的是多积累点功德，因为一年之初积累的功德是最大、最珍贵、最有意义的功德。人们会联合村里几家几户共同筹资为适龄的孩子们举办出家仪式。在仪式正式开始之前，准备出家的孩子都要身穿白衣，送到剃度的寺庙中，请住持僧人为他们念经祈福，再进寺庙给孩子剃发，穿裂装、听戒规，然后布施斋饭。新年出家的民俗也是在佛

185

教传入缅甸后演变成民间风俗，一直延续到今天。

洗头

　　为了抹去旧年的罪恶，青少年喜欢在泼水节或新年期间给年老的长辈们洗头、剪指甲。还有些人会敬奉长辈衣服、钱币、食品等布施物品。

三
老挝泼水节

　　泼水节是老挝隆重的节日，在每年的公历 4 月 13 日举行。节前人们就忙着赶集购买节日用品，进行舂米、酿酒、杀猪、宰牛、制火药、做高升、搭彩棚等节日准备。节日当天，男女老少身着传统服装，大清早就汇集到村头庙宇前的广场上，几乎全寨而出。10 多名年轻人有的戴面具，有的画上花脸，抬着自制的高升，敲锣打鼓、手舞足蹈，场面十分壮观。

　　泼水节的仪式简单而欢快，有些需要由寨子里最德高望重的老人主持。

　　第一项是传统的浴佛仪式。人们将水泼在佛像身上，为佛洗去灰尘，以此祈求佛祖对民众的保佑，帮人们祛病消灾。

第二项是放高升。老挝的放高升活动和中国傣族地区，特别是西双版纳傣族的放高升习俗有很多相同的地方。高升都是每家自制的，外面用彩纸和一些彩线加以装饰，这样看起来就十分漂亮。放高升需要一个空旷的广场，要搭建一个发射台。发射台是用竹竿或者木杆搭起来的约10米高的架子，作用是固定即将发射的高升。发射的时候，两个人将高升抬到发射台上，固定好以后由高升的主人点燃引线。随着一声巨响，高升会迅速窜上云霄。最远的能到达1000米之外。每放一次，都会受到群众热烈的欢呼。热情的人们将飞得最远的高升的主人抬起往上抛，以这样的方式来祝贺主人成功的制作与燃放。在老挝，放高升寄托着人们美好的憧憬，他们期盼着自己的生活能步步高升，也象征着勇敢、智慧和吉祥。

第三项就是泼水活动了。在家里吃过中午饭之后，每家每户的男女老少就会提着水桶、抬着盆，到泼水的广场开始泼水。在一阵阵激昂的鼓声中，青年男女提着装满清水的水桶互相追逐、嬉闹，把最清澈凉爽的水泼向对方，以这种方式来表达自己最好的祝福。在老挝人民的心中，水是大地的乳汁、生命的源泉。越是他们尊敬的人越应该被泼更多的水。泼水期间，也会有精彩的歌舞表演。老人们则会念经拜佛，祈福每年都风调雨顺、家人平安。

○全民狂欢的老挝泼水节（老挝南塔）

　　印度文明如源源不断的恒河水一样古老而神秘，尤其体现在其宗教上。印度有四大宗教，其中印度教在国内信仰的人数最多，影响也最为深远。印度的节日繁多，除了国庆节是政治性节日外，其他几乎都是宗教性质的。而其中最古老的便是印度教的"洒红节"，即泼水节。

　　泼水节源于印度，是古婆罗门教的一种仪式。在如今的印度，泼水节泼的是彩色的水，也就是"洒红"，顾名思义称为"洒红节"，也叫"胡里节""色彩节""霍利节"，是印度的传统节日，意味着印度传统新年的开始。最权威的说法是，洒红节源于印度的著名史诗《摩诃婆罗多》。

　　印度文化最显著的特色就是它的宗教性。宗教在印度文化起着举足轻重的作用，它塑造了印度人的人生观，与人们的生活息息相关。洒红节直接宣扬了信仰印度教会得到毗湿奴的保佑，正义最终将战胜邪恶。洒红节也与印度种姓密切相关。在印度的婆罗门（祭祀阶层）、刹帝利（武士阶层）、吠舍（农工商阶层）和首陀罗（奴隶阶层）四大种姓中，洒红节是首陀罗种姓的节日。这是一个低种姓的节日，一个平民的节日。虽然在法律制度上印度已经废除了种姓制度，但是这一陋习在印度人的心中仍有残留。在以前等级森严的社会中，种姓之间不可以通婚，各个种姓都有自己的分工，而且低种姓备受高级种姓的压迫和歧视。然而在这样一个节日中，男女老少，不分贵贱，都能尽情享受节日的欢乐。洒红节让印度底层人民暂时忘却种姓之间的尊卑，暂时忘却底层生活的压抑和无奈，充分地释放自己，尽情娱乐，彻底地放松。捉弄人和尽情欢乐是洒红节的精神所在，通常较低种姓的人将粉和颜料洒向高种姓的人，暂时忘记阶层的差异。这种备受宗教种姓制度压抑的人性在节日中被释放得淋漓尽致。

洒红节在印度历十二月（公历 2 ~ 3 月间）择日举行。这个节日也是印度的春节，代表着冬去春来，即新的一年的开始。过节期间，男孩们在街道上跳舞，人们向自己的朋好友，甚至是陌生人泼洒有颜色的粉末或者水。整个场面欢快而热烈。劲爆的音乐，欢乐的歌声，还有午夜的狂欢是这场盛会必不可少的部分。有些人会挨家挨户地去拜访，把颜料涂到老人的脚上或者直接泼洒到同辈的脸上、身上。在开始颜色盛会的前一晚，人们还会点起篝火，围着篝火嬉戏玩耍。夜晚，人们把用草和纸扎的霍利卡像抛入火堆中烧毁。印度人在洒红节期间还要喝一种乳白色饮料，据说可保来年平安健康。节日期间，人们互相抛洒花朵制成的红粉，投掷水球。水不仅仅是用桶、盆泼，还会用水枪喷射。被水枪喷射者仿佛跟掉进染缸里了一样。在北方邦的马图拉，除洒彩粉之外，妇女还要手持木棒追打男子，男子不能还手；在拉贾斯坦邦，人们则将浸水的衣服拧成一股绳，用来打人，被打者也不能还口、还手；在印度教圣地瓦腊纳西，人们互相洒水，然后成群结队上街游行，可以放肆地大声骂人；在比哈尔邦等地，民众还会唱歌颂春天，彼此甩泥巴、投牛粪。在广大农村地区，洒红节则更为热闹，有时庆祝时间长达一个多月。现在，洒红节已经演

189

变成人们消除误解和怨恨、摒弃前嫌、重归于好的节日。

　　泰国、缅甸、老挝、印度和中国的傣族等民族，虽然在泼水节中存在着习俗上的差异，但是各国人民都热爱生命、热爱生活，都通过水这一媒介来庆祝新的一年，祈求身体健康、吉祥如意。

Chapter Four

The Foreign Customs of the Water-Splashing Festival

Born in India and later adopted by Buddhism, the Water–Splashing Festival has become a traditional festival in South and Southeast Asian countries such as Thailand, Burma, Laos and India. But in different countries, the customs of the festival have big differences.

1. The Water-Splashing Festival of Thailand

Participating in the Water-Splashing Festival of Thailand in person, people's feelings may be very different. The Water-Splashing Festival, called in Thailand "Songkran Festival", is the most solemn traditional festival in Thailand. It is held from April 13 to April 15, lasting three days in succession, and has rich activities as monks'doing goodness, bathing the Buddha, worshipping the elders, float parade, singing and dancing, and freeing captive animals. But the most popular form people can see is "a national water fight".

The Water-Splashing Festival most prevails in Chiang Mai Province lying in northern Thailand and its surrounding provinces. On the eve of the festival, the streets are full of Thai national flags and prayer flags, and platforms are set up all along the streets. People have prepared water bottles, ladles, water guns and buckets for splashing water. Upon the arrival of April 13, the entire Chiang Mai becomes a watertown overnight. The main battleground is in the streets around the center of the city because there is a moat, which makes it very convenient to take water and replenish water at any time. Besides, there are also many pedestrians in the center of the city, which makes the festival extraordinarily noisy. Whenever pedestrians, motorcycles and cars pass by, people waiting along the streets will splash water towards them. The pedestrians will not walk far before they become drenched. The passing motorcycles and cars also "take a shower"; and people who ride and sit on motorcycles, needless to say, are all soaked through. If the car drivers are prepared, they will close the car windows, but buckets of water still fall from the sky. The driver's hatch is full of water, his view completely obscured, and the cars are trying to break through the "water array". If car windows are forgotten to be closed, the inside of the car will soon turn into a world of sea. In addition to the battle between people and the battle between people and cars, what is more interesting is the battle between cars. Water warriors sit on the pre-prepared "chariot" (a convertible buggy), provoking all through the streets, and by taking the chance of passing each other, they frantically pour over to the other party ladles of, basins of or buckets of water. The whole Chiang Mai is full of the spray of water, and the ground is deep in water. Laughter, crying, songs, cheers, and high-pitched honks of cars mix together, and every place has turned into a sea of joy.

On closer inspection, people splash water in different ways. There is the refined way of splashing water, with just a bottle of water splashing on the pedestrians; and the "barbarous" way, preparing a large basin of water and pouring with all strength to the people; and also the gentle way, in which lovers by the moat or in the park splash water. There, pairs of lovers, disregard of the fanatical water-splashing crowd, find a relatively devious corner, hug each other, and hold a water bottle each to splash water gently on the other's head. The water runs down from the top, soaking the whole body but also warming the whole body. In addition to splashing water for blessings, people also need to wipe the face with powder. During the days of the festival, every day there are people who wait on their own "battle field" in the street from the early morning and prepare respectively all kinds of water tools and face powder. As soon as someone passes by, they rush headlong to splash water and wipe the face powder. Not only the people being splashed are soaked through, but their faces become "painted faces". But no one would mind this, because it is a symbol of happiness and auspiciousness.

It is interesting to note that there seems to be particularly many girls riding a motorcycle in the street during the festival, and most of them "resolutely" rush to the "water array", which provokes the young men splashing water excitedly and hoppingly. They stop the girls on the motorcycle, and "pour" water on them and wipe the powder. This scene may arouse the complaint of newcomers who think that the young men have gone too far. But when seeing the girls being splashed and wiped not only unoffended, but also beaming with smiles and going on to the "trap", they find that it is a consensual and fair exchange, which is really interesting.

Of course, if meeting foreign visitors, people splashing water are usually polite enough to ask for their opinion before splashing water or wiping powder on them. Some foreigners also join the water-splashing crowd with water-splashing tools prepared beforehand, and they make more fun than the locals. Most foreigners do not participate in splashing water, instead they stand by and watch the fun. It is said that there was once a foreigner who was ignorant of the custom here, and was splashed "accidentally" when passing by the street on the day of the Water-Splashing Festival, which made him so angry that he complained to the relevant department, accusing the locals of "harassing" him. Unexpectedly, the complaint was rejected and the reason was simple: this is the biggest festival in Thailand, and the behaviour of the locals was not harassment, but being friendly.

The Water-Splashing Festival is a national carnival in

Thailand. During the festival, not only in cities, but in rural towns and remote villages far from the cities, people are all mobilised into the carnival. On both sides of the road from Chiang Mai to the ancient capital of Sukhothai, there can be seen along the road a vast water-splashing army dominated by young people, defending their "battle field" on the sides

Foreign visitors during the Water-splashing Festival in Thailand (Chiang Mai, Thailand)

of the road. Braving the scorching sun and a high temperature of more than 40 degrees, they are watching the people and cars passing by. Since there are not so many people and cars, and the car windows are mostly closed and the driving speed is very fast, it is not so easy to find the "target" of splashing water. Those who have participated in the Water-Splashing Festival in this region are always deeply impressed by the joyous and exciting view of the dark-skinned Thai children along the road who are holding water buckets and water guns, enduring the sun exposure, and wholeheartedly waiting for someone or cars passing by to splash water.

2. The Water-Splashing Festival of Myanmar

Compared with Thailand, the customs of the Water-Splashing Festival in Myanmar are more traditional and colorful. April 13 to 16 in solar calendar every year is the Water-Splashing Festival, the traditional festival of the Myanmar people greeting the Myanmar New Year. It is the most solemn and busiest time of the year for the Myanmar people.

There are different legends about the origin of the Water-Splashing Festival in Myanmar. The common one says that one year, the king of Myanmar saw immortals descending to the earth in the palace, which greatly pleased him. He made order to mix spices and water and splash on civil and military officials, signifying getting rid of the old and dirty and greeting the new year and good luck. According to the traditional belief in Myanmar, life is more or less sinful. It is believed that these sins can be washed away with clean water, which is to purify the soul and mind, so as to ensure a clean body at the dawn of the New Year. The people of Myanmar are mostly Buddhists, behaving modestly and courteously. But during the Water-Splashing Festival, they will vent themselves to the fullest, with young people indulging in drinking and singing from morning to night.

There are 12 months in the Myanmar calendar; each month not only has its name, but also has unique meaning; each month has a traditional festival. The first month of a year in Myanmar is called "Dagu", meaning the month of changing year and the beginning of the New Year, and the Water-Splashing Festival is held in this month. The Water-Splashing Festival is a grand nation-wide traditional festival in Myanmar, called in Myanmar "Dingjian". The word "Dingjian" originated from Sanskrit, meaning "transition, change, or transfer", namely, converting from the Old Year to the New

Year. The Water-Splashing Festival is the end of the Old Year in Myanmar calendar, so the Myanmar New Year is held on the last day of the festival. In order to wash away the dirt of the Old Year and usher in the New Year, people pour water on each other during the converting period. The period of the Water-Splashing Festival is the hottest time of the year in Myanmar, and the splashing of water symbolizes warmth, coolness and auspiciousness.

Calculated by month, the Myanmar calendar and the solar calendar are about three months apart. January 1 in the Myanmar calendar equals to April 16 or 17 in the solar calendar. The Water-Splashing Festival in Myanmar is usually held on April 13 to 16 in the solar calendar. Myanmar people believe the Water-Splashing Festival is the day when Indra, the god, comes to the human world to inspect the good or evil of humans, so the first day is the greeting day, the second day the arriving day, the third day the inspecting day, and the fourth day the returning day. Therefore, the Water-Splashing Festival usually lasts four days. During the festival, many local customs are presented.

Splashing Water

In Myanmar, April is the hottest season of the year. Celebrating the New Year by splashing water not only makes people feel the joy from the festival, but also brings a rare coolness to the hot summer days. Water during the Water-Splashing Festival is regarded by the Myanmar as a symbol of good luck and happiness, which can bring people good health. There is a folk saying that if someone is not splashed during the festival, and not wet by holy water of the festival, he or she will often get sick, while those who get wet by the holy water

197

of the festival will not get sick. But during the Water-Splashing Festival, three types of people will not be splashed: one is the monks wearing saffron robes, another is the elderly, and the third is pregnant women. In Myanmar, there are two ways of splashing water, the gentle way and the wild way. The gentle way, which is also the traditional way, is to use the fragrant cherry branches to dip clean water with sandalwood or perfume in the silver bowl, and gently splash on other people. Such a method is now rare, only for some leaders or distinguished guests. As for the wild way, it is mostly done between the young people. The modern Myanmar Water-Splashing Festival involves people walking or riding along the roads to be splashed by others. People like to pour the whole buckets or basins of water; some people even spray with a hose. And the water splashed is often melted ice water from ice blocks, so when poured on the body, it will chill to the bone. But those being poured will not get angry; the more people get splashed, the happier they will be. In addition, people, regardless of gender, occupation, identity and even the degree of familiarity, can splash water on each other. Nowadays, many people in big cities prefer to attend the festival by riding open-topped cars to the water-splashing station.

Once April arrives, on both sides of each city's main streets in Myanmar, many temporary stages, also known as water stations, which are set up by the voluntary organization of citizens or enterprises or by the government, suddenly spring up. Some are grand and magnificent, others are small and exquisite, but their common feature is to pour water on the pedestrians and vehicles passing by. Around water stations, the carnival scene of young people can be seen everywhere:

in the centre of the stage young men and women are singing and dancing; they hold all kinds of plastic water guns, dancing joyously and infatuatedly; they stand on the convertible trucks, singing and dancing, venting themselves to the fullest and unscrupulously. On the open-air stage of the water stations, Myanmar girls in festive costumes are dancing joyously the traditional dances. Other young men on the stage take pipes to spray water on the spectators. On the street-oriented side of the stages, some people are holding water pipes to spray water onto the passing crowds and cars. The convertible water-splashing trucks, one after another, slowly pass the water-splashing platforms in turn; the people in the trucks are more willing to stay under the stage longer and willingly accept the cool blessing. The more people get splashed, the happier they will be, for water symbolizes happiness. The modern Myanmar Water-Splashing Festival has been completely dominated by wild splashing way.

Dancing

In Myanmar, two months before the Water-Splashing Festival, singing can be heard everywhere; in big cities or small villages, people can hear the joyous songs from every household. People can not only hear the most famous traditional Water-Splashing Festival songs by Mandalay Muma Orchestra such as "Dubo Dubo", "Mandalay flowers", "The rain of the Water-splashingFestival", and "Getting shelter from Mandalay Hill". Other happy modern dance music also covers the whole period of the Water-Splashing Festival. During the festival, regardless of urban or rural areas, on every decorated tent temporarily set up, beautiful girls are dancing the traditional water-splashing dances of Myanmar. There are various performances on the open-air stages, inclucling beautiful group dances and fashionable modern dances.

Offering Food

On the first day of the New Year, Myanmar people like to make all kinds of snacks. The activity held in various places to donate food is called "Studitha", which comes from Sanskrit, meaning "all directions", namely, people from all directions are welcome to participate. The organizers will provide free food (usually traditional snacks) to each participant. The most representative snack is the "water-splashing rice dumplings". Sometimes young people will put hot peppers or coins in the dumplings for fun. It is lucky to get the dumpling with a coin, but even if someone eats the one with hot pepper, he or she will not get angry, and it will be over in laughing and joking. Famous traditional food also includes "Winnowing the fish", which is a kind of cold drink made from agar and sweet water. People shape short strips from rice noodles, and add coconut gravy and brown sugar water or sugar water while eating. There are also some people who make a lot of snacks at home, inviting relatives and friends to pay a visit, or sending to neighbors or relatives. So at the dawn of the New Year, offering food becomes a traditional custom of Myanmar.

Sending New Year Flowers

Myanmar in April is immersed in a world of water and flowers. At this time, there is a flower called "red sandalwood flower" blooming coincidentally during the Water-Splashing Festival. Red sandalwood flower is the national flower of Myanmar, petite, pale yellow, not gorgeous, but blooming only once a year, and blooming only one day on time once, so the Myanmar people cherish this holy flower that blooms only once a year. Before the New Year, there is always a rainfall. There is usually no rain three to four months before April, but upon the arrival of the New Year, it suddenly starts to rain. The first rain is called New Year rain, after which the red sandalwood flowers in whole Burma bloom. The flowers respected by the Myanmar people bring vitality to the whole country, and with their unique fragrance, deliver New Year's greetings and hope to the people of Myanmar. When the red sandalwood flowers blossom, every Myanmar woman will arrange some flowers on the head. Upon looking, it is a world of yellow, so breath of the Water-Splashing Festival can be felt through the flowers. The red sandalwood flower is a symbol of Water-Splashing Festival in Myanmar. It is also a love letter for young men and women; because it blooms only once a year, people regard it as a metaphor for fidelity and faith in love. The young man will pick up the red sandalwood flower from the tree and give it to the girl he likes, and the girl's accepting it and inserting into her hair shows that she has accepted the boy's pursuit.

Abstinence

The Water-Splashing Festival is the most celebrated holiday among the traditional Myanmar festivals. It is not only the time for people to entertain themselves, but also a good period of doing good deeds. During the Water-Splashing Festival, there is the saying of changing-year inspection in Myanmar, which is a legend evolved after Buddhism being introduced to Myanmar and also a legend evolved from the fusion of Buddhism and Myanmar folk customs. It is said that the Jade Emperor sent envoys to inspect people for their vice and virtue. The envoys floated down from the sky on New Year's eve to inspect the world, holding golden pattra leaves in one hand,

and a dog-skin book in the other. The good men were recorded in the golden pattra leaves, while the wicked in the dog-skin book. So the Myanmar like to observe the five commandments or eight commandments during the Water-Splashing Festival, and go to the Buddhist temples or the pagodas to worship the Buddha and chant sutras. Myanmar people believe in Buddhism piously, and observing the five commandments is a daily practice, which include no killing, no stealing, no lying, no offending another person's wife or daughter, and no drinking. During the Water-Splashing Festival, people usually go to the temple to observe the eight commandments, which, on the basis of the five commandments, have another three commandments as no sitting or sleeping on the tall and luxuriant bed and no dressing up, no listening to the music and no dancing, no eating food and only drinking water from 12 at the noon to 5 the next morning. It is usually the elderly people who go to the temple to observe the commandments and listen to the Buddha to explain the Buddhist scriptures, religious cultivation, the practice and so on. There are also people who bring their children or grandchildren to the temple to do the good.

Bathing the Buddha

Bathing the Buddha is held on the first day of the Water-Splashing Festival. People offer flowers, incense and candles in their own Buddhist prayer room, then do "bathing the Buddha" with clean water, that is, washing dust away from the Buddha statue. The goal is to pray for the welfare of the whole family and everlasting peace year after year. There are also some people who participate in the activity of bathing the Buddha in the temple .

Freeing Captive Animals

After the four-day Water-Splashing Festival, the Myanmar New Year begins. Early on the first day of the New Year, the government usually holds a ceremony of freeing captive animals in the park, symbolically freeing cattle and sheep. Ordinary people also buy live fish to be killed and free them in the river or the fish pond in the temple. In order to do good deeds, freeing captive animals has become a New Year custom of the Myanmar people, who can free not only live fish, but also live birds.

The Ceremony of Becoming a Monk

Parents like to send their sons to the temple to be novice monks during the Water-Splashing Festival to show their sincere devotion to the Buddha. Becoming a monk is the biggest event in the life of Myanmar people, and boys can become adults only after they have become monks. It is a glorious thing to send the children to the temple. In Myanmar, the boys' retreat life in the temple can be long or short; the shortest may be a week before secularization, and becoming a monk again is allowed for further retreat later, with unlimited number of times, and some may be monks for life; the longer may be several months or years. All the boys in Myanmar love to become monks during the Water-Splashing Festival, which usually lasts five days from the greeting day to the New Year Day. People become monks especially during the New Year for good luck, the purpose of which is to accumulate more merits, and the merit accumulated at the beginning of the year is the biggest, the most precious, and the most meritorious. Several families in the village raise money together to hold the ceremony for the eligible children. Before the ceremony officially begins, the children who are to become monks will be clothed in white and sent to the tonsure temple. The Buddha are asked to pray for them. And then in the Buddhist temple, they will have their hair shaved, dress in the burnt orange robes of the monks, and listen to the religious precepts, and then offer vegetarian food. Becoming a monk during the New Year has also evolved into a folk custom after Buddhism was introduced to Myanmar, and cotinues till today.

Washing Hair

To erase the evil of the Old Year, teenagers like to do acts of kindness, for example, washing hair or trimming nails for the elderly people during the Water-Splashing Festival or New Year. Some people also revere the elders by offering them clothes, money or food.

3. The Water-Splashing Festival of Laos

The Water-Splashing Festival is a grand holiday in Laos, held on 13th April in solar calendar every year. Before the festival, people are busy buying at the fair holiday supplies, making such preparations for the festival as pounding rice, making wine, slaughtering pigs and cattle, making gunpowder and Gaosheng, and setting up decorated tents. On the day of the festival, people without reference to age and sex, dressed in traditional costumes, rally in the square in front of the temple at the end of the village early in the morning, nearly all the villagers out. A dozen of young people, some wearing masks, some with painted faces, carry Gaosheng made by themselves, beating drums and gongs, dancing joyously. The the scene is quite spectacular.

The rituals of the Water-Splashing Festival are simple and

lively, and some need to be hosted by the most respected elders in the stockade.

The first is the traditional ritual of bathing the Buddha. People splash water on the Buddha statue to wash away the dust from the Buddha, praying for the Lord Buddha's blessings to the people and helping people to ward off diseases and evils.

The second is letting off Gaosheng. There are a lot of common items for letting off Gaosheng in Laos and that in Dai areas in China, especially Dai nationality in Xishuangbanna. Gaosheng is home-made, with its appearance decorated by coloured paper and colorful threads, which makes it look very beautiful. Letting off Gaosheng needs a spacious square to set up a launch pad with bamboo poles or wooden poles, which is about 10 meters high and designed to keep in place Gaosheng ready to be launched. Before launch, two men rise up the Gaosheng to the launch pad, keep it in place, and then its master will light the fuse. With a blare, the Gaosheng will quickly soar into the sky, among which the farthest can reach more than 1000 meters. Every letting off will be cheered enthusiastically by the crowds. The enthusiastic people lift and throw up the master of the Gaosheng that flies the farthest to congratulate the master's successful making and letting off. In Laos, letting off Gaosheng presents people's beautiful vision for future that their lives will rise higher and higher. It also symbolizes bravery, wisdom and auspiciousness.

The third is the water-splashing activity. After lunch at home, people of each household will carry buckets or basins to the splashing square to splash water. In waves of passionate drums, young men and women, carrying buckets full of water, chase and play with each other, splashing the clearest and coolest water on each other, and in this way expressing their best wishes. In the heart of the Lao people, water is the milk of the earth and the source of life. The more people are respected, the more they should be splashed. There will also be great singing and dancing performances during the Water-Splashing Festival. The elderly will chant and worship the Buddha, praying for good harvest and family safety every year.

The Water-Splashing Festival in Laos (Luang Prabang, Laos)

4. The Water-Splashing Festival of India

Indian civilization is as old and mysterious as the endless stream of Ganges, especially presented in its religion. There are four major religions in India, and among them Hinduism has the most believers and the deepest influence at home. There are many festivals in India; except for the National Day being a political festival, the rest are nearly all religious, with the oldest being Hindu "Splashing-red Festival", that is, the Water-Splashing Festival.

The Water-Splashing Festival originated from India and is a ritual of the ancient Brahmanism. In today's India, the water splashed during the Water-Splashing Festival is colorful water, that is, "splashing red"; as its name implies, "Splashing-red Festival", also called "Holi Festival", "Color Festival" or "Holi", is India's traditional festival, which indicates the beginning of the traditional New Year in India. The most authoritative statement is that Splashing-red Festival originated from India's famous epic *Mahabharata*.

The most striking feature of Indian culture is its religious nature. Religion plays a very important role in Indian culture, which has shaped Indian people's outlook on life and is closely related to people's life. Splashing-red Festival directly advocates that those who believe in Hinduism will be blessed by Vishnu, and that justice will eventually prevail against evil. The festival is also closely associated with the Hindu caste. In the four Indian castes of Brahman (sacrifice caste), Kshatriya (warrior caste), Vaisya (agricultural, industrial and commercial caste) and Sudra (slave caste), Splashing-red Festival is a festival for Sudra caste. This is a low-caste festival, a festival for civilians. Although India has abolished the caste system in the legal system, this corrupt custom is still deeply rooted in Indian people's mind. In the strictly hierarchical society, the intermarriage between different castes is not allowed, each caste has its own division of labor, and the low castes are greatly discriminated and oppressed by the high castes. However, in such a festival, people, without reference to age and sex, regardless of their descent, can all fully enjoy the happiness of the festival. Splashing-red Festival makes Indian people in the bottom strata temporarily forget superiors and inferiors between castes, and temporarily forget the depression and helplessness of life, and fully release themselves, playing hard and completely relaxing. It is the spirit of Splashing-red Festival to play tricks on people and make merry. Usually people of lower castes spray powders and paints to those of higher castes, temporarily forgetting the distinctions of castes. The release of human nature greatly repressed by religious caste system is fully explained in the festival.

Splashing-red Festival is held in December (February to March in the solar calendar) of the Indian calendar. This festival is also India's Spring Festival, meaning the passing of winter and coming of spring, that is, the beginning of the New Year. During the festival, boys dance in the streets; and people are pouring colour powder or water to their friends and even strangers. The whole scene is joyful and enthusiastic. The music of strong beats, the singing of joy, and the midnight revelry are essential to the event. Some people pay a visit from door to door, painting the paints on the elderly's feet or splashing directly onto the peers' face or body. One night before the colour pageant, people will start a bonfire and play around it. At night, people throw Holika figures made of grass and paper into the fire to burn them up. Indians will also drink a kind of white milky drink during the festival, which is said to ensure peace and good health for the upcoming year. During the festival, people throw red powders made from flowers and water balls to each other. Water is not only splashed with buckets or basins, but also with water guns. Those who have been splashed by water guns are like falling into a dye vat. In Mathura of the state of Uttar Pradesh, besides splashing colorful powders, women will also hold a wooden stick to chase and beat men, while men cannot hit back; in the state of Rajasthan, people wring the soggy clothes into a rope to beat people, and the victim cannot retort or hit back; in Varanasi, a Hindu holy site, people splash water on each other and then go to the streets in droves to parade, and at that time swearing at people loudly is allowed; in places such as Bihar, people will also sing songs to extol spring, throwing mud or cow dung at each other. In the vast rural areas, the festival is more lively, and sometimes the celebration will last more than a month. Now, Splashing-red Festival has evolved into a festival when people eliminate misunderstanding and resentment, disregard previous enmity and are reconciled to each other.

Although custom differences on the Water-Splashing Festival exist in Thailand, Burma, Laos, India and Dai nationality in China, people all over the world show their passion for life; and through water, they celebrate the New Year and pray for good health and good luck.

结　语

　　民族节日是一个民族风土人情、宗教信仰、历史传统和道德伦理等文化因素的高度凝练，是一个民族历史文化的长期积淀和活态化石，也是一个民族传统文化的生动展示。随着时间的推移，它成为深深植根于祖国大地上的一种文化现象，也是一座亟待挖掘的文化宝库。作为民族文化的载体，民族传统节日映射出民族文化发展的历程，它随着时间、自然环境、社会历史的变迁而转型。变迁是一切文化的永存现象，也是文化发展的必然。泼水节作为一扇了解民族文化的"窗口"，随着时代的进步、旅游业的发展和外来文化的不断介入，这扇"窗口"也无形中吸纳着外来文化的因子，发生了

○ 欢迎参加我们的泼水节（昆明—芒市航班上）

211

前所未有的变化。可以说，当今的"泼水节"所处的历史时代和环境已经远远超出了所谓的"传统"范畴，迈入了现代社会经济发展的大环境之中，特别是在旅游场景中，"泼水节"更是被赋予了时代的特色。正因如此，"泼水节"在现代社会中的传承与发展开拓了一条新的发展之路。

一个民族节日的起源最初都是单一的，从相关的民族调查资料和老人的口述中可以发现，泼水节作为一种民俗活动，最初完全由民间自发的形式进行，甚少受到外界力量的干预。而在其传承、深化和发展变迁的过程中，却不断从单一化向多元化演化。随着时代的进步和发展，泼水节的内容也越来越丰富起来。

对于区域性的民族传统节日而言，早些时候进行节日准备时，囿于生活水平的原因，节日的安排往往比较单一，除了基本的器物准备，几乎没有娱乐活动。现在对于节日的准备内容显然更加丰富了，除了添置新衣服、打扫卫生、准备祭拜供品外，人们还要准备各种表演的娱乐性节日。娱乐活动除了在本村寨节日期间表演外，还有可能被邀请去其他村寨参加联谊，甚至被邀请到市州上参加演出。不仅如此，泼水节的社会参与主体也越来越多元。除了当地的傣族及相关的其他民族，还有作为活动组织者的政府、旅游部门、从事旅游开发的各种企业单位、从中央到地方的各级新闻媒体、各界专家和学者以及慕名而来的中外游客。

毫无疑问，泼水节已经从简单的节庆功能延伸为展现傣族水文化、音乐舞蹈文化、饮食文化、服饰文化和民间传说等传统文化的综合符号，这将"泼水节"搬上了更大的空间领域和舞台，使"泼水节"具有了标志性符号而使其社会功能变得更加强大。

可以说，过去的"泼水节"在民族文化中是传承与发展的重要内容，而现在的"泼水节"本身已被时代赋予了更为丰富的内涵。

变迁中的它更充分说明了，它既是传统的，也是现代的；既是民族的，
更是当代大众的。

Conclusion

A national festival is the high condensation of a nationality's culture factors including the local conditions and customs, religious beliefs, historical traditions and moral ethics and so on. It is the long-term accumulation and living fossil of a nation's history and culture, and is also a vivid display of its traditional culture. Over time, it has become a cultural phenomenon deeply rooted in the earth and a cultural treasure house waiting to be rediscovered. As a carrier of national culture, the traditional festivals of a nationality reflect the development history of national culture and will experience transition with the change of time, natural environment and social history. Change is the perpetuating phenomenon of all cultures and the inevitability of cultural development. The Water-Splashing Festival, as a "window" to know national culture, with the progress of the era, the development of tourism and the growing involvement of foreign culture, is virtually absorbing the factors of foreign culture, and has experienced unprecedented changes. So to speak, the historical era and environment of "the Water-Splashing Festival" today have gone far beyond the scope of so-called "tradition", and have entered the broad environment of economic development of modern society. "The Water-Splashing Festival" in the scene of tourism is even more so endowed with characteristics of the times. Just because of this, a new way of development has been opened up for "the Water-Splashing Festival" in modern society.

The origin of a national festival is initially single. From the related national survey data and the elders' oral account, it can be found that Water-Splashing Festival, as a kind of folk activity, initially proceeded completely by spontaneous organization of the people, and got little interference by outside powers. But in the process of its inheritance, promotion and development, it has evolved continuously from singularization to diversification. With the progress and development of the times, the contents of Water-Splashing Festival have become more and more abundant.

For the regional traditional festival of a nationality, at the time of preparing for the festival earlier, limited by living standards, festival arrangements usually tended to be simple: there were almost no entertainment activities except for basic objects. Now, preparations for the festival are obviously more abundant; in addition to buying new clothes, cleaning, and preparing worship offerings, people will also prepare various entertainment performances. And entertainment activities, besides being performed at the village during the festival, may also indude being invited to make friendly contacts in other villages and even being invited to perform in the city or the prefecture. Not only that, the social participants of the festival are more and more diverse. In addition to the local Dai people and other related ethnic groups, there are also the government as the organizer, the department of tourism, the various business units engaged in tourism development, news media from central to local level, experts and scholars from all walks of life, and admiring tourists at home and abroad.

Without doubt, the Water-Splashing Festival has extended from a simple festival function to a synthetic symbol displaying the traditional culture of Dai nationality such as water culture, music and dance culture, food culture, costume culture, folklores and so on. "Water-Splashing Festival" has been uplifted to a bigger space and stage, taking on an iconic symbol with stronger social functions.

Happy children (Jinghong, Yunnan Province)

So to speak, "Water-Splashing Festival" in the past is an important part of the heritage and development of the national culture, while "Water-Splashing Festival" at present has been endowed by the era with more abundant connotation. Being in change more fully illustrates that it is both traditional and modern, both national and international.

附　录　Appendix

菠萝饭的制作方法
The Cooking Method of the Pineapple Rice

　　菠萝饭，又叫凤梨饭，是傣族的一种特色美食，在营养全面，富含维生素及蛋白质，有助于提高记忆力；它外形可爱，色彩丰富，香甜可口，很受广大食客们的欢迎。

　　Pineapple rice, also called bromeliad rice, is a kind of special food of Dai nationality. With comprehensive nutrition and rich vitamins and protein, it can improve our memory. Looking lovely, colorful and sweet, it is greatly welcomed by diners.

材料：
1. 原料：菠萝一个、糯米 200 克；
2. 配料：青豆、虾仁、胡萝卜、白砂糖。
Ingredients：
1. Raw materials: one pineapple, glutinous rice 200g;
2. Ingredients: green beans, shelled shrimps, carrots,sugar.

使用厨具：电饭煲或蒸锅。
Cooking utensil: rice cooker or cooking pot.

制作步骤 /Procedures

1. 糯米，提前泡 2 个小时，青豆、虾仁泡发，胡萝卜洗净、切丁；

1.Glutinous rice, soaked for two hours beforehand; green beans and shelled shrimps, soaked; carrots, washed clean and diced;

2. 泡好的糯米放入蒸锅蒸熟；

2.Steam the soaked glutinous rice in cooking pot;

3. 菠萝洗净外皮，顶部切掉一小块当盖子，挖空里面的菠萝肉，切成小块；

3.Clean the outer cover of the pineapple, cut a small piece from the top to be the lid, scoop the flesh inside and cut into dices;

4.将青豆、虾仁、胡萝卜丁，以及少量菠萝肉块一起翻炒，炒制半熟；
4.Stir-fry green beans, shelled shrimps, carrot dices and a small amount of pineapple flesh cubes to be half-cooked;

5.糯米饭蒸好后晾凉，在米饭里拌上白糖，与青豆、虾仁、胡萝卜丁、菠萝肉块拌匀；
5.Cool the steamed glutinous rice, and mix with sugar, green beans, shelled shrimps, carrot dices and pineapple flesh dices thoroughly;flesh cubes to be half-cooked;

6.拌好的米饭及配料装入菠萝盅里；
6.Put the mixed glutinous rice and ingredients in the pineapple cup;

7. 盖上菠萝盖子隔水蒸 15 分钟；
7.Put the pineapple lid on, and steam for 15 minutes;

8. 端上桌，打开菠萝盖子，一份香喷喷的菠萝饭大功告成！
8.Put on the table, open the pineapple lid, and an appetizing pineapple rice is done!

丛书后记

　　上下五千年的悠久历史孕育了灿烂辉煌的中华文化。我国地域辽阔,民族众多,节庆活动丰富多彩,而如此众多的节庆活动就是一座座珍贵丰富的旅游资源宝藏。在中华民族漫长的历史长河中,春节、清明、端午、中秋等传统节日和少数民族节日,是中华民族优秀传统文化的历史积淀,是中华民族精神和情感传承的重要载体,是维系祖国统一、民族团结、文化认同、社会和谐的精神纽带,是中华民族生生不息的不竭动力。

　　春节以正月为岁首,贴门神、朝贺礼;元宵节张灯、观灯;清明节扫墓、踏青、郊游、赏牡丹;端午节赛龙舟、包粽子;上巳节祓禊;七夕节乞巧,牛郎会织女;中秋节赏月、食月饼;节日间的皮影戏、长安鼓乐;少数民族的节日赶圩、歌舞美食……这一桩桩有趣的节日习俗,是联络华人、华侨亲情、乡情、民族情的纽带,是中国非物质文化遗产的"活化石"。

　　为了传播中华民族优秀传统文化,推进中外文化交流,中国人类学民族学研究会民族节庆专业委员会与安徽人民出版社合作,继成功出版《中国节庆文化》丛书之后,再次推出《多彩中国节》丛书。为此,民族节庆专委会专门成立了编纂委员会,邀请了国际节庆协会(IFEA)主席兼首席执行官史蒂文·施迈德先生、中国文联原执行副主席冯骥才先生、第十一届全国政协民族和宗教委员会副主任周明甫先生等担任顾问,由《中外节庆网》总编辑彭新良博士担任主编,16位知名学者组成编委会,负责丛书的组织策划、选题确定、体例拟定和作者的甄选。

出版《多彩中国节》丛书，是民族节庆专业委员会和安徽人民出版社合作的结晶。安徽人民出版社是安徽省最早的出版社，有60余年的建社历史，在对外传播方面走在全国出版社的前列；民族节庆专业委员会是我国节庆研究领域唯一的国家级社团，拥有丰富的专家资源和地方节庆资源。这套丛书的出版，实现了双方优势资源的整合。丛书的面世，若能对推动中国文化的对外传播、促进传统民族文化的传承与保护、展示中华民族的文化魅力、塑造节庆的品牌与形象有所裨益，我们将甚感欣慰。

掩卷沉思，这套丛书凝聚着诸位作者的智慧，倾注着编纂者的心血，也诠释着中华民族文化的灿烂与辉煌。在此，真诚感谢各位编委会成员、丛书作者、译者以及出版社工作人员付出的辛劳，以及各界朋友对丛书编纂工作的鼎力支持！希望各位读者对丛书多提宝贵意见，以便我们进一步完善后续作品，将更加璀璨的节庆文化呈现在世界面前。

为了向中外读者更加形象地展示各民族的节庆文化，本丛书选用了大量图片。这些图片，既有来自于丛书作者的亲自拍摄，也有的来自于民族节庆专委会图片库（由各地方节庆组织、节庆主办单位报送并授权使用），还有部分图片是由编委会从专业图片库购买，或从新闻媒体中转载。由于时间关系，无法与原作者一一取得联系，请有关作者与本书编委会联系（邮箱：pxl@jieqing365.com），我们将按相关规定支付稿酬。特此致谢。

《多彩中国节》丛书编委会
2018 年 3 月

多彩中国节
泼水节

Series Postscript

China has developed its splendid and profound culture during its long history of 5000 years. It has a vast territory, numerous nationalities as well as the colorful festivals. The rich festival activities have become the invaluable tourism resources. The traditional festivals, such as the Spring Festival, the Tomb-Sweeping Festival, the Dragon Boat Festival, the Mid-Autumn Festival as well as the festivals of ethnic minorities, represent the excellent traditional culture of China and have become an important carrier bearing the spirits and emotions of Chinese people, a spirit tie for the national reunification, national unity, cultural identity and social harmony, and an inexhaustible motive force for the development of Chinese nation.

The Spring Festival starts with Chinese lunar January, when people post pictures of the Door Gods and exchange gifts and wishes cheerfully. At the Lantern Festival a splendid light show is to be held and enjoyed. On the Tomb-Sweeping Festival, men and women will worship their ancestors by sweeping the tombs, going for a walk in the country and watching the peony. And then the Dragon Boat Festival witnesses a wonderful boat race and the making of zongzi. Equally interesting is the needling celebration on the Double Seventh Festival related to a touching love story of a cowboy and his fairy bride. While the Mid-Autumn Festival is characterized by moon-cake eating and moon watching. Besides all these, people can also enjoy shadow puppet shows, Chang'an drum performance, along with celebration fairs, songs and dances and delicious snacks for ethic groups. A variety of festival entertainment and celebrations have formed a bond among all Chinese, at home or abroad, and they are regarded as the "living fossil" of Chinese intangible cultural heritage.

In order to spread the excellent traditional culture of China, and promote the folk festival brand for our country, the Folk Festival Commission of the China Union of Anthropological and Ethnological Science (CUAES) has worked with the Anhui People's Publishing House to publish *The Colorful Chinese Festivals Series*. For this purpose, the Folk Festival Commission has established the editorial board of *The Colorful Chinese Festivals Series*, by inviting Mr. Steven Wood Schmader, president and CEO of the International Festival And Events Association (IFEA); Mr. Feng Jicai, former executive vice-president of China Federation of Literary and Art Circles(CFLAC); Mr. Zhou Mingfu, deputy director of the Eleventh National and Religious Committee of the CPPCC as consultants; Dr. Peng Xinliang, editor-in-chief of the Chinese and foreign Festival Website as the chief editor; and 16 famous scholars as the members to organize, plan, select and determine the topics and the authors.

This series is the product of the cooperation between the Folk Festival Commission and Anhui People's Publishing House. Anhui People's Publishing House is the first publishing house in Anhui Province, which has a history of over 60 years, and has been in the leading position in terms of foreign transmission. The Folk Festival Commission is the only organization of national level in the field of research of the Chinese festivals, which has experts and rich local festival resources. The series has integrated the advantageous resources of both parties. We will be delighted and gratified to see that the series could promote the foreign transmission of the Chinese culture, promote the inheritance and preservation of the traditional and folk cultures, express the cultural charms of China and build the festival brand and image of China.

The Colorful Chinese Festivals Series is bearing the wisdoms and knowledge of all of its authors and the great efforts of the editors, and explaining the splendid cultures of the Chinese nation. We hereby sincerely express our gratitude to the members of the board, the authors, the translators and the personnel in the publishing house for their great efforts and to all friends from all walks of the society for their supports. We hope you can provide your invaluable opinions for us to further promote the following works so as to show the world our excellent festival culture.

This series uses a large number of pictures in order to unfold the festive cultures in a vivid way to readers at home and abroad. Some of them are shot by the authors themselves, some of them come from the picture database of the Folk Festival Commission (contributed and authorized by the local folk festival organizations or organizers of local festival celebrations), and some of them are bought from Saitu Website or taken from the news media. Because of the limit of time, we can't contact the contributors one by one. Please don't hesitate about contacting the editorial board of this series (e-mail: pxl@jieqing365.com) if you're the contributor. We'll pay you by conforming to the state stipulations.

Editorial Committee of *The Colorful Chinese Festivals Series*

March, 2018